Indoor Gardens
Living with Plants

My own lounge is well furnished with groups of foliage plants, and with specimens such as yucca and palms. Splashes of colour are provided by flowering plants.

Indoor Gardens
Living with Plants

Alan Toogood

Salem House Publishers
Topsfield, Massachusetts

ACKNOWLEDGEMENTS

The publishers are most grateful to Mr and Mrs A. Toogood, Mr and Mrs A. Billitt, Mrs B. Potter and Frederika Davis for allowing us to visit their homes to photograph their houseplants.

The colour photographs on pp. 2, 7, 10, 17, 27, 33, 65, 85, 89 and 93 were taken by Bob Challinor; those on pp. 47 and 48 were taken by Hugh Palmer.

The publishers are grateful to the following persons and agencies for granting permission for reproduction of the colour photographs: Hugh Palmer (p. 15); Frederika Davis (pp. 57, 61 and 79); J. Becker/Zefa (pp. 28 and 41); B. Baert/Vision International (pp. 44, 117 and 123); Michael Boys Syndication (pp. 21, 25, 51 and 73); Elizabeth Whiting & Associates (pp. 69, 99, 103, 107, 111, 113 and 125).

All the line drawings were drawn by Rosemary Wise.

First published in the United States by Salem House Publishers, 1986, 462 Boston Street, Topsfield, MA 01983.

Library of Congress Catalog Card Number: 86-60677

ISBN: 0 88162 200 1

Printed and bound in Italy by G. Canale and Co SpA

CONTENTS

PREFACE

There are many books on houseplants so why, might you ask, have I written another? Well, this one embraces not only houseplants, but many other kinds, too.

My aim is to encourage you to make far more use of your home for growing plants: not only the normal rooms, but also balconies, enclosed porches, and even cellars and cupboards with no natural light.

I have endeavoured to show you that many other kinds of plants can be grown indoors, apart from the normal houseplants, like fruits and vegetables; that many plants can be raised indoors for later planting outside, perhaps in the garden or on the balcony; and that tender plants and vegetables and fruits can be stored for the winter in the house.

The book should, I hope, be especially encouraging to people who do not have gardens, for it demonstrates that a wide range of gardening activities can be undertaken with only the rooms of the house or flat, and perhaps a balcony, at one's disposal. The ideas are equally applicable, of course, to garden owners.

I have assumed little or no prior knowledge of gardening – in other words, I have included all the basic information necessary for successful cultivation, but at the same time I have been progressive, so more knowledgeable gardeners should find plenty to interest them.

As you can see from the title, two distinct areas have been covered – general gardening indoors and displaying houseplants. I have chosen to deal with houseplants in this particular way because I feel that so little attention is given to displaying them attractively. Many books give only the briefest of guides and therefore it is little wonder that so many people have no idea of the possibilities open to them.

Not only have I included the normal, better-known ways of displaying plants, but also many unusual, very attractive, methods, too. Some of the ideas are my own, developed over the years, while others have been gleaned from houseplant enthusiasts whom I have visited during the preparation of this book. Among the ideas for displaying houseplants effectively you will find suggestions for bold specimen plants, mixed groups, elevating plants, climbers, making use of walls, growing plants on 'trees', making maximum use of windows, growing plants in glass fish tanks, creating miniature gardens, growing moisture-loving and water plants and growing plants without soil (hydroponics).

I have also discussed the use of artificial lighting, both for display work and for raising and growing plants. Many people like to have houseplants in their offices but come up against various difficulties in respect of choice and cultivation, so I have tried to solve these problems.

There is a wealth of houseplants to choose from, but many people limit their choice to the well-known favourites. However, some of the more unusual kinds can be just as easy to grow, so I have deliberately included a good range of these. New houseplants appear on the market each year, so I have described all the recently introduced ones, indicating this where applicable.

Basically, this is an ideas book, but I have not neglected the practical side: basic cultural needs for each plant are given; and there are chapters on general care of houseplants and propagation of house- and other plants. There is also a run-down on the tools and equipment you are likely to need for indoor gardening.

The photographs and drawings illustrate the ideas for growing and displaying and have been specially commissioned for my book. I hope they inspire you – that is my aim.

A.T.

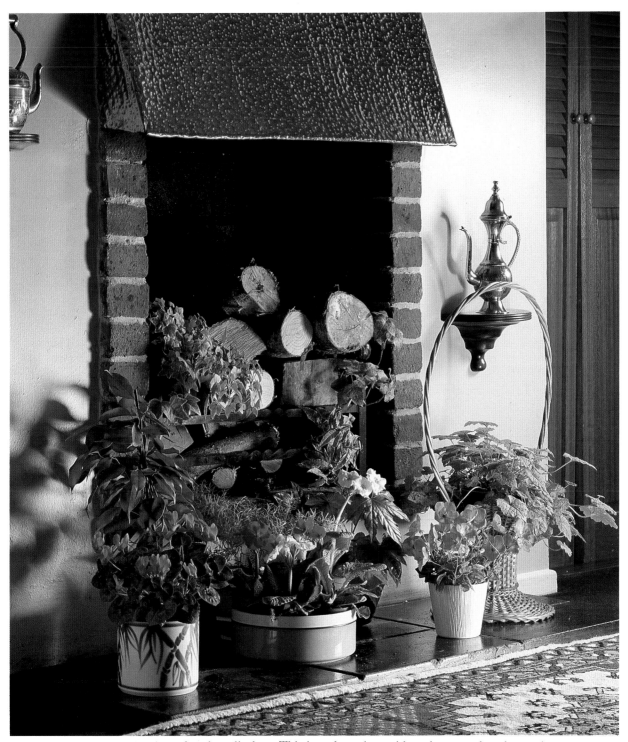

I use my fireplaces for plant displays. This is early spring, with cyclamen, polyanthus and *Campanula isophylla* in flower, and a foil of *Ficus benjamina*, ivies, asparagus ferns and fatsia.

1
TOOLS AND EQUIPMENT

Comparatively little is required in the way of tools and equipment for indoor gardening and care of houseplants. Certainly not every item which I have listed below is considered essential: some are classed as 'luxury' items, the sort of things which often make welcome presents for indoor-gardening enthusiasts.

Watering can   This, of course, is essential as you cannot accurately water plants with, say, a milk bottle! Choose an indoor watering can, small and light in weight, and with a long spout for reaching plants which are high up or at the back of plant groups.

Hand pressure sprayer   There are many of these available from garden centres, and I consider one an essential item of equipment. It is used for mist spraying plants to provide humidity around them, and also for applying insectides and fungicides. Ideally have one for misting and another for applying pesticides. They need only be small – about 0.5 litres (1 pint) capacity.

Secateurs   These are used for pruning and for removing dead flowers. You will need only a lightweight pair for indoor gardening, ideally choosing a model with narrow pointed blades. Alternatively, you might find a pair of flower scissors more useful and these will probably be cheaper than secateurs.

Hand fork and trowel   These are not really essential, as old table forks and spoons would be equally suitable! It is possible to buy small versions of hand forks and trowels for indoor gardening. The fork is generally used for loosening the surface of compost and often assists in dividing plants. A trowel is used for planting, for handling potting compost, etc. Probably these tools are more useful for balcony gardening where plants are often grown in large containers (see Chapter 2).

Thermometer   This may be considered a luxury item, although there is no denying it is useful for checking that the rooms of the house have sufficient warmth for your plants. Ideally buy a maximum-minimum thermometer which indicates the highest and lowest temperature in a 24-hour period (day-time and night-time temperatures). An ordinary thermometer simply indicates the present temperature in a room.

Soil-moisture meter   If you are inexperienced in watering plants this may well prove extremely useful. It consists of a metal probe which is pushed down into the compost or soil to ascertain the moisture content. There is a calibrated dial at the top which will indicate 'wet', 'moist' and 'dry'.

Light meter   This can be useful but is not essential. It accurately measures the amount of light (it's far more accurate than the human eye in this respect). It can spring a few surprises – that 'bright' corner in your living room may well have very poor light conditions. As you will see in following chapters, it is important to provide plants with optimum light conditions.

Hygrometer   This is a meter for measuring the humidity (moisture content) of the atmosphere. It is not considered an essential piece of equipment, even though many plants need humid conditions. Provided you ensure humidity, as indicated in the chapter on plant care, you do not really need to measure it. However, a hygrometer would make an acceptable present, perhaps.

Fertilizer   Absolutely essential, for all plants need feeding on a regular basis. Available in various forms, the most popular being concentrated liquid fertilizer. There are also powdered fertilizers for dissolving in water, and fertilizer tablets which are inserted in the compost or soil, where they release their plant foods over a period of several weeks, ideal if you are inclined to forget to feed plants.

Leaf-shine products These are not essential, but they are used to enhance the natural shine of thick-leaved foliage plants. They can give a rather unnatural appearance. Regularly sponging off the leaves of plants with plain water will keep them looking shiny and healthy.

Insecticides and fungicides You should have these in readiness for any attacks by pests and diseases. Buy a proprietary houseplant insecticide which controls most of the pests commonly encountered. Some come in convenient aerosol form. At the time of writing there is no fungicide specifically for houseplants, for controlling diseases like mildew and grey mould (botrytis). So I would suggest you buy a small pack of the general-purpose fungicide, benomyl.

Composts You will need a range of these, but do not stockpile them, for they deteriorate if kept for too long. They are best bought in small amounts and used straight away. There is a choice of soil-based (John Innes) and peat-based or soilless seed and potting composts. The latter are widely used, but some plants are better in JI composts, as indicated in appropriate chapters. Some composts are dual-purpose, being suitable for seed sowing and potting. There are composts, too, specifically made for houseplants.

You will not be able to buy cutting composts, which you will need if you go in for plant propagation. However, a suitable compost is easily mixed at home, and consists of equal parts by volume of peat and coarse horticultural sand or grit; both are readily available in small packs from garden centres. If you are growing lime-hating plants you will need to buy a proprietary ericaceous compost, which is free from lime or chalk.

Pots and containers You will need a selection of pots, of course. Plastic ones are suitable for the majority of plants, but others are better in clay pots, and this is indicated where appropriate in other chapters. More specialized containers are also included in appropriate chapters.

Propagating case This is highly recommended if you want to raise plants from seeds and cuttings. Ideally, invest in one of the small, electrically heated windowsill propagating cases, which are very cheap to run. There are unheated versions available, these being more suitable for summer propagation, when conditions are naturally warmer.

Polythene bags Clear polythene bags are often used instead of propagating cases (Chapter 23).

Hormone rooting powder This is highly recommended for treating cuttings to ensure successful rooting (Chapter 23).

More specialized equipment and accessories are included in other chapters as applicable.

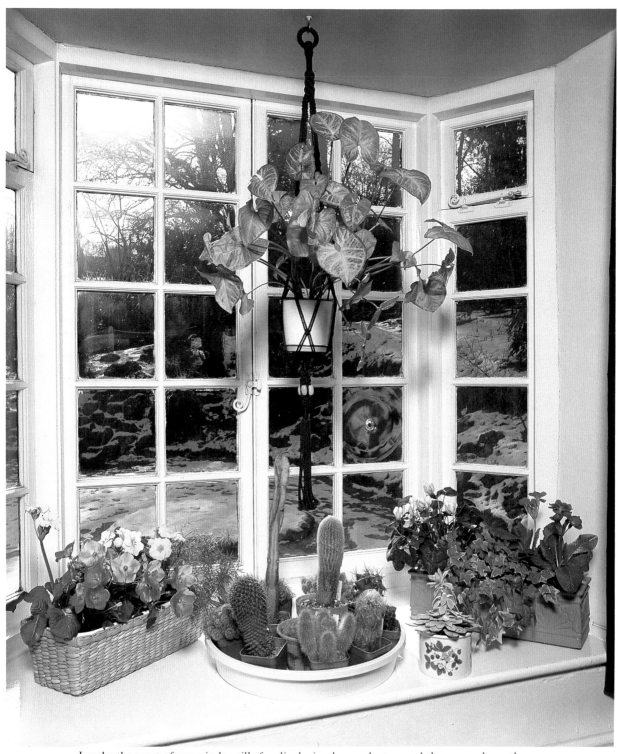

I make the most of my windowsills for displaying houseplants—and the space above them.
The plant in the hanging macrame container is a syngonium or goosefoot plant.

Part 1

GARDENING ON BALCONIES AND IN PORCHES

2
BALCONY GARDENING

If your flat or house has a balcony it is sensible to make maximum use of it for growing plants, perhaps utility kinds as well as ornamental subjects. A colourful balcony can give an enormous amount of pleasure, not only to yourself but also to passers-by, if it is at the front of the house or flat. For many people, of course, growing plants on a balcony is the only form of outdoor gardening they can indulge in, but as will be revealed, it is surprising just how many different kinds of plants can be grown, with a little thought. Even vegetables and fruits should not be dismissed.

CONDITIONS ON THE BALCONY

As with any garden, a balcony can have a few problems, but these are generally easy to solve. One of these problems is wind. Some balconies, especially on very high buildings, can be very windy, so do consider some form of wind-break.

Trellis screens could, perhaps, be erected on the windward side or sides to filter the wind. You could, for example, use timber trellis panels, which come in various heights. Generally they are supplied treated with cedarwood preservative but if not do be sure to treat them yourself; or, you may prefer painted trellis, perhaps white or pale grey.

Trellis-work makes an ideal support for climbing plants and these further help to filter the wind. Such screens also give privacy from adjacent balconies.

Instead of trellis screens for wind protection, transparent plastic panels could be used, either clear or tinted, or even frosted if you want privacy also. Such panels are often used on roof gardens, but they are just as suitable for the edges of balconies.

Unless balconies project well away from the building, lack of light can be a problem, especially with the type of balcony that has a 'roof' overhead – in other words, one that is set well back into the building. The light can be very poor at the back of such balconies but nevertheless would be suitable for many plants which do not mind shade, like fuchsias (perhaps trained as standards, fans or other shapes), begonias, polyanthus and bay trees in pots. Certain houseplants which prefer shade could be staged at the back of dark balconies for the summer. The front or outer edges of such balconies should be reserved for plants which need maximum light and even sun. More about plants later.

CONTAINERS AND COMPOSTS

All plants will have to be grown in containers of one kind or another but fortunately there are plenty to choose from.

Window-boxes
Generally the back wall of a balcony has a window or two, and good use should be made of these by installing window-boxes.

They can be bought, of course, and are available in timber, fibreglass or plastic. Window-boxes can also be placed on top of balcony walls but in this instance they must be securely fixed by means of metal brackets, and they may need drip trays underneath them.

You may also be able to make your own timber window-boxes, designing them to fit exactly the width of the windows or a particular length of balcony wall.

It is necessary to ensure that window-boxes retain moisture, so it is recommended that their minimum depth and width is 25 cm (10 in). To ensure that surplus water is able to drain away, the boxes should ideally have a slight gap beneath them. They must, of course, have drainage holes. Wooden boxes can be painted to match the colour of the windows, but if you do not wish to do this then at least treat them with a clear horticultural wood preservative to prolong their life.

Hanging and wall baskets

You should make maximum use of wall space, too, by installing some hanging baskets, supported with suitable ornamental brackets, perhaps in black-painted wrought iron. Baskets could also be hung from the 'ceiling' at the front of the balcony. For balcony work I would advise using the solid moulded-plastic baskets which have a built-in drip tray – especially if the baskets are to be hung at the front.

There are available, too, special half-circular baskets and other containers which are designed for fixing directly on to walls. These are ideal for making maximum use of wall space.

Pots and tubs

Visit any good garden centre and you will find that there is a very wide range of pots and ornamental tubs available in all sizes. These will form one of the main ways of growing plants on a balcony. However, a word of caution here: many are very heavy and therefore quite unsuitable for balconies. You must not subject a balcony to extreme weight. Therefore containers which are to be stood on the floor should be very light in weight, made from plastic or fibreglass. Do ensure, too, that they have drainage holes in the base.

Ordinary plastic flowerpots come in a very wide range of sizes, but consider, too, ornamental urns and tubs, as well as shallow bowls. Rectangular troughs give great scope for planting, as do the large square, rectangular or round 'planters' (simply large deep containers).

The proprietary plastic Tower Pots (available from a supplier in the UK), are highly recommended for balconies (Fig. 1). Basi-

cally they consist of a tall cylinder with planting 'pockets' protruding from the sides. They were originally designed for growing strawberries (and what better way of growing these fruits on a balcony?) but can also be used for other subjects, such as colourful summer bedding plants.

Parsley pots, too, are ideal for balconies, not only for parsley but for other herbs and small plants such as alpines or rock plants. They are generally jar-shaped and have holes in the sides, in which plants are inserted.

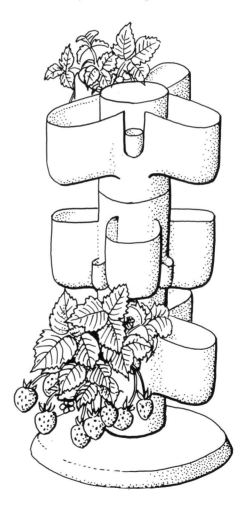

Fig. 1. Many plants can be grown in a small area if proprietary plastic Tower Pots are used. Although designed for growing strawberries, they can also be used for other plants, like colourful summer bedding.

13

Growing-bags

A boon to the balcony gardener must surely be the growing-bag. This is a long (generally 1.2 m or 4 ft) plastic bag filled with light-weight peat compost. Growing-bags can be used for all kinds of plants and they are temporary, generally being used only once for any one crop – vegetables, for example. Very good growth is possible in bags, provided the plants are well fed and watered. They do not dry out as quickly as pots. Normally drainage holes are not made in the bottom of growing-bags, but if you find that rain is making the compost too wet, then it would be advisable to provide drainage holes. In this instance the bags could be placed on shallow plastic gravel trays containing light-weight horticultural aggregate, to catch surplus water. There are available, too, special growing-bag crop supports to support tall plants such as tomatoes. These are usually made of plastic-coated steel and have special 'feet' which are placed under the bag.

Composts for containers

For filling containers which are to be stood on the floor of the balcony I would strongly advise using the all-peat composts which are very light in weight. These can also be recommended for window-boxes and hanging baskets. There is a very wide range of proprietary all-peat potting composts available. You have to be rather careful with watering, though, for it is very easy to apply too much with the result that the compost remains wet – peat-based composts dry out more slowly than soil-based types. Also you have to ensure they do not dry out completely, for when in this state they are very difficult to moisten again.

BALCONY GREENHOUSES

Balcony gardeners need not be deprived of a greenhouse for there are special small models available for balconies. There is a very wide range, too, at least in the UK, of mini-greenhouses. Both types are very small – you cannot actually get inside them, but work from the front through sliding doors or panels. These greenhouses are ideal for growing crops of tomatoes, aubergines, capsicums, etc., and they can also be used for plant raising in the spring.

If you are at all worried about the weight problem on your balcony, then consider a greenhouse clad in plastic rather than glass, as this is very much lighter in weight. An aluminium-framed greenhouse is also lighter than one with a timber frame, such as western red cedar.

The greenhouse should be placed in the lightest possible part of the balcony, in sun ideally. If you find that the sun is too strong for the plants in the summer, then you can provide shading by 'painting' the glass with a proprietary liquid greenhouse shading material. Do not use this on plastic. Alternatively place a sheet of muslin over the greenhouse during periods of hot sunshine, removing it when the sun has passed off.

There is no reason why a mini-greenhouse should not be heated in the winter to keep it frost-free, so that you can overwinter tender plants. For example, it could be fitted with electric air-warming cables, which are mounted on the inside walls, or a small electric tubular heater could be used. Do keep a check on temperature, though, for a tiny greenhouse can quickly become too hot for plants. Provide ventilation as necessary. This also applies in the spring and summer when conditions are naturally warm – on a sunny day the temperature inside can become dangerously hot so that plants may be damaged. Ventilate freely in warm or hot weather. A thermometer installed inside will allow you to keep a check on temperatures.

CARE OF BALCONY PLANTS

On a balcony you should pay particular attention to watering, for sun and wind can quickly dry out the compost in containers. Remember that containers dry out very much more quickly than soil in a garden. So it pays

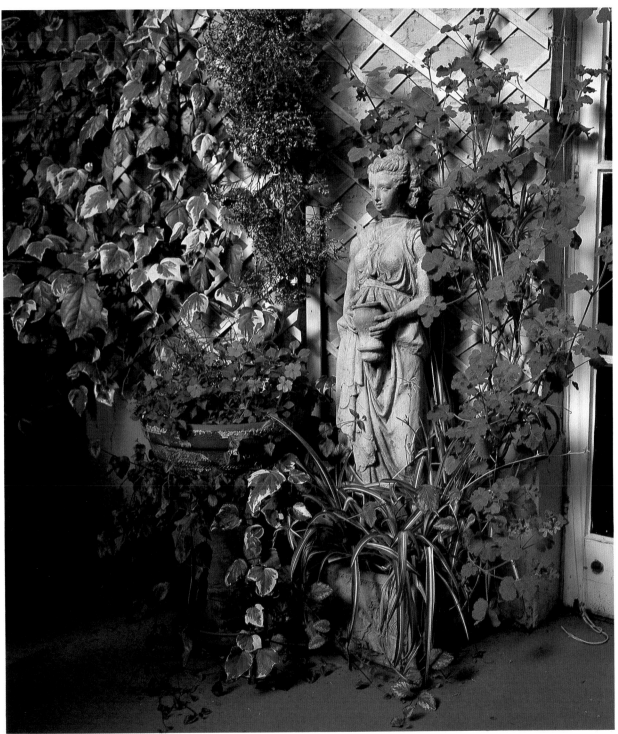

An attractive balcony, with trelliswork for climbers like variegated ivy. Tender impatiens and pelargoniums are providing colour. Statuary for a balcony must be light in weight.

to check all containers at least daily, especially in warm weather. Even twice daily would not be too frequent in hot conditions. When the compost is becoming dry, watering should be thorough so that the entire depth of compost is moistened. This means applying sufficient so that it actually runs out of the drainage holes in the bottom. In the case of growing-bags without drainage holes you can check the depth of penetration by pushing a finger down into the compost.

Plants in containers need regular feeding during the growing period – spring and summer – for they quickly use up the plant foods in the compost. Most gardeners will prefer to use a liquid fertilizer, this being applied about once a fortnight, according to the maker's instructions. Use a general-purpose liquid fertilizer, or a tomato fertilizer, high in potash, for tomatoes, capsicums, aubergines and other fruiting plants. Start feeding newly planted subjects only when they are well established in their containers, which will be a matter of eight weeks or so.

Whenever you are preparing containers for planting (apart from growing-bags and hanging baskets) always place a layer of drainage material in the bottom first, such as a 2.5 cm (1 in) layer of crocks (broken clay flower pots) or lightweight horticultural aggregate. This should cover the entire bottom of the container. Do make sure the container has adequate drainage holes. Top the drainage layer with some rough peat and then add the compost. Peat-based composts must not be firmed too much – follow the instructions on the bag.

If you are growing temporary plants in containers, such as spring and summer bedding plants, then bear in mind that the compost is best replaced every two or three years with fresh compost.

Permanent plants, such as hardy shrubs, may be started off in small pots and moved into larger containers as they grow. This is better than planting a small specimen in a large container for it will have too much compost around its roots, which is liable to

remain wet. So be prepared to pot on permanent plants in the early spring, just before they start into growth. Generally plants are potted on by two sizes – for example, from a 15 cm (6 in) pot to a 20 cm (8 in) pot.

Permanent plants which are well-established in final containers will from time to time need a change of compost. This can be achieved by re-potting into the same container. First the plant is removed and some of the old compost teased away from the roots – about 5 cm (2 in) from the sides, top and bottom of the root ball. A little root pruning could also be carried out to slightly reduce the size of the root system. Then the plant is put back into the same container, filling in with fresh compost. The best time to do this is when the plants are dormant, say in late winter. Repotting is generally needed about every two years.

In the years between repotting, the plants should be top-dressed with fresh compost. In the spring, scrape off 2.5–5 cm (1–2 in) of the old compost from the surface and replace with fresh.

PLANTS FOR THE BALCONY

It is possible to have colour and interest on a balcony all the year round, perhaps using a combination of hardy and tender plants. The balcony can also be productive, in that vegetables and fruits can be grown.

Spring and summer bedding plants
These are the first choice of most people for containers, such as tubs, window-boxes and hanging baskets.

Trailing kinds of summer bedding are ideal for the edges of containers and for hanging baskets, such as trailing lobelia, ivy-leaved pelargoniums, trailing varieties of fuchsia, petunia and tuberous begonia, alyssum and trailing verbena. More bushy summer bedding plants include ageratum, gazania, impatiens, mesembryanthemum, mimulus, nemesia, nicotiana, bedding dahlias, petunia, salvia, French and African

Another part of my lounge where good use is being made of wall space. Trellis panels support pot-holders so the plants can be quickly re-arranged or replaced.

marigolds, fibrous-rooted and tuberous begonias, *Cineraria maritima*, bush fuchsias, heliotrope and pelargoniums. Most need sun, but impatiens, lobelia, begonia, cineraria, and fuchsias will grow and flower well enough in a shady spot.

Include with these summer bedding plants some tender, permanent plants in pots, which can be overwintered indoors. Simply stand them out on the balcony from early summer to early autumn. Interesting subjects for this treatment include *Abutilon striatum* 'Thompsonii', large yellow-mottled leaves; *Agave americana* 'Marginata', with its rosette of yellow-edged sword-like leaves; *Chlorophytum comosum* 'Variegatum', the spider plant, with grassy green and white striped foliage; *Coleus blumei* varieties, with multicoloured leaves; *Cordyline australis*, with narrow grey-green foliage; and *Echeveria glauca*, a succulent, forming a rosette of greyish leaves.

Remember that all summer bedding plants are tender and should only be planted outside when all danger of frost is over, which is by late spring to early summer in Britain.

Spring-flowering bedding plants for tubs, window-boxes and other containers include *Bellis perennis* 'Monstrosa', the double daisy; *Cheiranthus cheiri*, the wallflower; *Cheiranthus allionii*, the Siberian wallflower; myosotis or forget-me-not; polyanthus, and winter-flowering pansies (viola). Bellis, myosotis, polyanthus and pansies will succeed in shade. Plant spring bedding in autumn.

Bulbs

There are many hardy spring-flowering bulbs for containers (like tubs and window-boxes), including chionodoxa, crocuses, galanthus or snowdrops, hyacinths, muscari, narcissus (daffodils), scillas and tulips (both dwarf and tall varieties). Galanthus and narcissus can be successfully grown in shade. Spring-flowering bulbs are planted in the autumn although tulips can be planted in late autumn. Bulbs such as hyacinths and tulips can be planted among spring bedding plants if desired to make a really colourful show.

Permanent hardy plants

If you want some permanent hardy plants for balcony tubs and planters make a choice from shrubs and herbaceous perennials.

Suitable shrubs, which do not grow too large, include *Acer palmatum* 'Atropurpureum'; *Camellia japonica* varieties (need acid compost); *Chamaecyparis lawsoniana* 'Ellwoodii', a slow-growing conifer; *Laurus nobilis*, the sweet bay, making a good clipped specimen; dwarf evergreen azaleas like the Kurume hybrids, and dwarf rhododendrons such as *R. yakushimanum*, both needing acid compost; and yuccas. All but yuccas can be successfully grown in partial shade.

Do not forget a few climbers, too: some which can be grown in large tubs include the large-flowered clematis hybrids, which like their roots in shade and their stems in sun; the winter jasmine, *Jasminum nudiflorum*, for sun or shade; the honeysuckle, *Lonicera periclymenum* 'Belgica'; and the hardy grape vine, *Vitis* 'Brant', which produces edible black grapes and needs full sun.

Herbaceous perennials which are suitable for tubs and planters include agapanthus; hemerocallis hybrids, which tolerate partial shade; hostas, which also tolerate shade; and phormiums or New Zealand flax, which will be happy in partial shade or full sun.

As we are a nation of rose-lovers it would be absurd not to have a few on the balcony, growing in tubs or planters. Choose the lower-growing kinds of large-flowered (hybrid tea) and cluster-flowered (floribunda) bush roses, with heights and spreads of 45 to 75 cm (18–30 in). Less vigorous climbing roses, like 'Golden Showers' and 'Aloha', which attain only about 1.8 m (6 ft) in height, are suitable for tubs and, like other climbing plants, can be trained to trellis-work. The miniature roses are ideal for window-boxes and smaller tubs. All roses need plenty of sun.

Vegetables

A wide range of vegetables can be grown in growing-bags. Larger vegetables, like tomatoes, capsicums (sweet peppers), aubergines and outdoor cucumbers, can alternatively be grown in 30 cm (12 in) pots. Other vegetables which are particularly suited to growing-bags include dwarf French beans, round-rooted beetroots, round- or stump-rooted carrots, endive, lettuce, spring or salad onions, dwarf early peas and radishes.

Remember that the tender vegetables – tomatoes, capsicums, aubergines and outdoor cucumbers – must not be planted outside until late spring, when all danger of frost is over. Of course, if you have a balcony greenhouse this would be the place to grow them. They can be planted in this in mid spring.

Some culinary herbs are ideal for container growing. As they are perennial, they could be grown permanently in 30 cm (12 in) pots. A good selection includes mint, chives, rosemary, sage and thyme. Parsley is popular, too, but is raised anew each year from seeds, sown in spring. It can be grown in parsley pots – those with holes in the sides. Herbs are best grown in sun but they will tolerate partial shade. Few tolerate deep or permanent shade, although mint will flourish.

Fruits

Now that it is possible to buy dwarf bush trees, growing fruits in containers is very much a practical proposition. They do need full sun, though, and can be grown in 30–38 cm (12–15 in) pots to start with, although eventually they will need a final size of 45–60 cm (18–24 in) in diameter and depth.

Buy fruit trees from a fruit specialist and ensure they are on dwarfing root-stocks, and are therefore suitable for containers. With apples and pears you will need several different varieties to ensure cross-pollination. Alternatively, buy a 'family' tree, with several varieties on the one tree, perhaps an even better choice for the limited space on the balcony.

If you want to grow a cherry buy the self-fertile variety 'Stella', on the dwarfing 'Colt'

root-stock. The plum variety 'Victoria' is also self-fertile, and should be bought on the dwarfing 'Pixy' root-stock. Bush peaches can be grown singly, such as varieties 'Hale's Early' or 'Duke of York', but you must hand-pollinate the flowers, using a soft artist's brush. Figs can be grown as bush trees and grapes can be grown as standards, in other words, on a single straight stem with a head of branches at the top, each winter the current year's shoots from the head being cut back to within one bud of their base.

You may wish to grow citrus fruits, too, like the sweet orange, *Citrus sinensis*, and the Seville orange, *C. aurantium*. They can be grown as bush trees but as they are tender they must be moved indoors for the winter. Grow them in full sun.

Fruit trees must be pruned, of course, but as this varies from one type to another, and is quite involved, I would refer readers to a specialist text book on fruit growing.

Strawberries are probably the easiest of the fruits to grow on a balcony, and are best grown in Tower Pots (see p. 13). Strawberries can also be grown in growing-bags but should be given a new bag each year. The time to plant strawberries is late summer.

Houseplants

Balcony gardeners could place some of their houseplants outside for the summer. Of course, this applies only to the tougher and more hardy subjects, many of which actually benefit from a spell out of doors, making far better growth.

Plants which can be placed outside include chlorophytum, coleus, × fatshedera, fatsia, hederas, bromeliads, iresine, *Campanula isophylla*, *Citrus microcarpa (C. mitis)*, hydrangea, impatiens, jasminum, pelargoniums, *Rhododendron simsii*, and cacti and succulents. Some of these, particularly the foliage plants and the cacti and succulents, could perhaps be grouped with summer bedding plants to create an 'exotic' corner on the balcony.

3
GARDENING IN PORCHES

The front, or rear, doors of many houses are protected by means of enclosed porches which often make ideal temporary or permanent homes for plants.

The type of porch which I have in mind has a solid front and sides to a height of about 1 m (3 ft), maybe of timber or brickwork. The rest is glass, except for the roof which may be solid (not allowing light to enter), but in some porches the roof is made from transparent corrugated PVC, in which case the porch will be very light indeed. Even if porches do not have a transparent roof they are generally very light places – they often face a sunny aspect.

So generally there is no problem with lack of light. Indeed there may be too much sun – in the summer the small area can heat up rapidly unless the door is kept open. You may have to protect plants from direct sun, as sun shining through glass can seriously damage them. One way of achieving this is to hang net curtains at the windows and to draw them during hot sunny conditions.

A glassed-in porch provides shelter from wind, from cold winter weather and may even protect plants from all but the most severe frosts. That is, provided it is well sealed. So if you want to grow plants in your porch check all joints etc., and seal them as necessary. Do not forget to put draught-excluder around the door if required.

Many people treat enclosed porches almost like mini-greenhouses and fill them with plants – a welcome sight for visitors. It is possible to have interest and colour all the year round if you use a combination of hardy and tender plants. Certainly a glassed-in porch gives you another 'room' for plants.

Do bear in mind that plants can dry out very rapidly in summer when the weather is hot, so keep a daily eye on water requirements. Tender plants, though not all, will need removing from the porch in autumn and overwintered in a warmer room indoors.

A CHOICE OF PLANTS FOR PORCHES

Hardy plants

These can be used mainly to provide interest and colour during the winter, when most of the tender plants will have been moved into a warmer room indoors. There are both flowering and foliage plants which will overwinter well in porches.

Particularly suitable are alpines or rock plants grown in pans of gritty compost, like John Innes potting compost No. 1 to which has been added one-third extra of grit or coarse sand.

Many of the popular alpines found in garden centres flower in the winter and spring, like the huge range of saxifrages, some of the gentians, *Pulsatilla vulgaris*, *Primula allionii*, iberis and *Alyssum saxatile*. The pans of plants are best put out of doors after flowering, or in a well-ventilated cold frame, and moved back into the porch in autumn.

I also like to buy a few winter-flowering heathers for my porch, varieties of *Erica carnea*, like 'Springwood Pink' and 'Springwood White'. They flower for months on end. Again, place them outdoors after flowering.

Any of the hederas or ivies are suitable for providing foliage interest in the winter, as they are hardy. They can be grown as trailers or climbers.

The hardy foliage shrub, *Fatsia japonica*, is

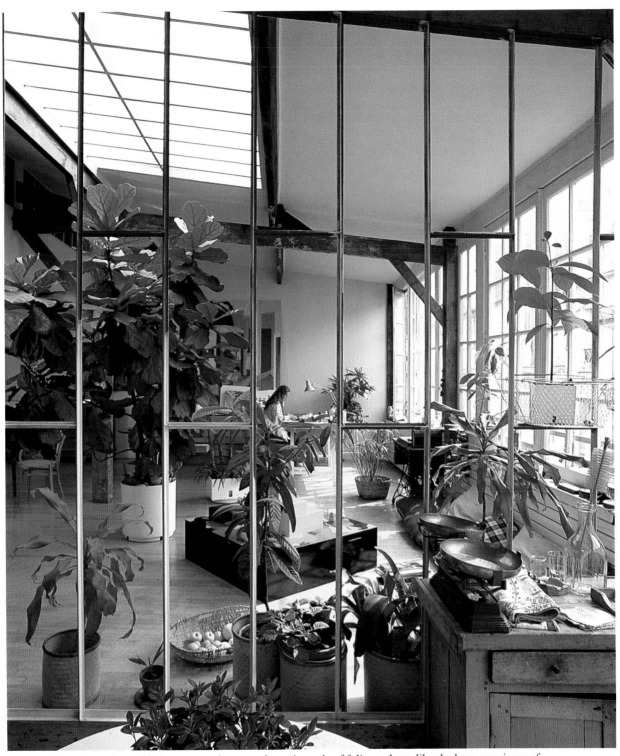

A continental living room where much use is made of foliage plants like the huge specimen of the fiddleback fig, *Ficus lyrata*.

21

an excellent porch plant, with huge hand-shaped glossy green leaves. Eventually it will become too large, but could then be planted in the garden. The same comment applies to another hardy foliage shrub, *Aucuba japonica*. However, for a few years, while young, it can be pot grown to furnish the winter porch with greenery. I suggest you choose varieties with yellow-mottled leaves, like 'Crotonifolia', 'Gold Dust', 'Picturata' and 'Variegata'.

For bright flower colour I can strongly recommend polyanthus, potted into 12.5–15 cm (5–6 in) pots in the early autumn. Also, rather similar, are the coloured pot primroses which are becoming so popular. They are available in a wide range of colours and have an extremely long flowering season. Polyanthus and primroses can be bought from most garden centres.

Spring-flowering bulbs

These are also hardy – the hyacinths, narcissus (daffodils), tulips and large-flowered Dutch crocuses. They look particularly attractive when grouped with other hardy plants, like polyanthus, primroses, hederas and aucuba.

The bulbs are planted in early autumn, using bulb bowls, which do not have drainage holes, and proprietary bulb fibre, which consists basically of peat. There are various-size bulb bowls available, most popular being those with a diameter of 15 cm (6 in). This size of bowl will comfortably hold two to three large bulbs of hyacinths; or one top-sized daffodil; or five tulips; or eight crocuses. Plant one variety of bulb per container. When planting bulbs in bowls the tips are left exposed above compost level. Do not use specially treated bulbs for porches (which flower in time for Christmas) as they need artificial heat to bring them into early flowering.

When planting, first place a layer of bulb fibre in the bottom of the bowl, then stand the bulbs on it. Fill in with more fibre and firm it lightly with your fingers. Water in after planting and then provide the bulbs with a period of complete darkness and cool conditions. Keep in a temperature below 9°C (48°F). For example, put the bulbs in a dark cellar. Alternatively, enclose each bowl in a black polythene bag and place in a cool shady place out of doors. The traditional method is to bury the containers under 10–15 cm (4–6 in) of peat or sand in a cool shaded part of the garden. Ensure the compost is kept moist, so check occasionally.

After a period of about eight weeks, when the bulbs have produced roots, and shoots are about 2.5 cm (1 in) high, remove them from these conditions and put in the porch. Flowering will take place in late winter or spring, several weeks in advance of bulbs in the garden. After flowering plant the bulbs in the garden as they are not suitable for container-growing again.

Tender pot plants

It is amazing just how 'hardy' some of these are, for I have found that there are several subjects which can remain in an unheated porch over the winter, provided the compost is kept almost dry between late autumn and early spring. Examples include *Acacia dealbata*, citrus fruits, fuchsias, eucalyptus (such as *E. globulus*), pelargoniums, *Campanula isophylla*, *Araucaria heterophylla (A. excelsa)*, *Asparagus densiflorus* 'Sprengeri', *Cissus antarctica* and *C. rhombifolia*, and *Saxifraga stolonifera*.

The following pot plants I have found particularly useful for providing colour in spring, summer or autumn. Of course, they should be moved into a room indoors for the winter if there is risk of them being damaged by severe frosts.

Achimenes flower in summer, in a wide range of colours, and are grown from rhizomes potted in the spring. These can be kept from year to year. The calceolaria or slipperwort has brilliant pouched flowers and is a short-term pot plant, being discarded after flowering.

The same is true of the dwarf pot chrysanthemums which can be bought in flower at any time of the year, the blooms lasting for many weeks. Cyclamen are surprisingly hardy and flowering starts in the autumn and continues into winter. I particularly like the new miniature varieties.

Greenhouse fuchsias are indispensable for summer colour and can be kept from year to year when, of course, the plants will become larger. The same applies to the florists' hydrangea, the mop-headed type, although most people will treat it as a temporary pot plant. It can be bought in flower in spring or summer.

The impatiens, or busy lizzies, thrive in the porch and should be given a shady spot if possible, and certainly abundant supplies of water during the summer flowering period.

Like fuchsias, pelargoniums are essential summer-flowering porch plants – the regals, zonals and ivy-leaf varieties, the latter with a trailing habit of growth. They can be kept for several years, or renewed annually from cuttings. Long-term pot plants are the azalea hybrids (*Rhododendron simsii*), virtually hardy, flowering in autumn and continuing into winter. For summer flowering try streptocarpus, which can be kept for a number of years, but give them a rest during the winter.

4

RAISING PLANTS

It is possible to raise, or start off, indoors, plants for growing out of doors – in the garden or on balconies and in porches. It is common practice to raise such plants as summer bedding and tender vegetables on a warm window-sill indoors for later planting out. Many people do this because they do not own a greenhouse, or because their greenhouse is not sufficiently warm due to the high cost of heating. Such tender plants have to be raised in warmth but once they are well established they can be transferred to a greenhouse if you have one (provided they can be kept free from frost), before finally being planted in the open.

If possible tender plants should be hardened off (gradually acclimatized to outdoor conditions) in a garden frame for a few weeks before planting out, but this stage will have to be skipped if you are not a garden owner. At least try to 'harden' the plants to outdoor conditions on a window-sill by opening the windows during favourable weather to ensure airy conditions, but at all costs avoid subjecting the plants to cold draughts.

For plant raising indoors you will need a window-sill propagating case to provide bottom heat (see Chapter 1). Poor light conditions can be a problem when raising things like bedding plants and tender vegetables indoors early in the year, often resulting in weak, spindly seedlings which will never make strong sturdy plants.

RAISING SUMMER BEDDING PLANTS FROM SEEDS

These are sown early in the year and planted outside when all danger of frost is over – late spring to early summer generally being con-

sidered safe. Some need to be sown very early, as they are slow growers, others later in the spring as they quickly grow and come into flower. Examples are as follows:

Sow in midwinter: antirrhinum, *Begonia semperflorens*, calceolaria (shrubby bedding type), dianthus, lobelia, pelargonium, pyrethrum.

Sow in late winter: *Centaurea gymnocarpa*, dahlia (dwarf bedding types), felicia, gaillardia, gazania, heliotropium, impatiens, matricaria, mesembryanthemum, nemesia, nicotiana, petunia, *Phlox drummondii*, salvia, verbena.

Sow in early spring: ageratum, alyssum, callistephus, cosmea, mimulus, tagetes (French, African and Afro-French marigolds), *Tagetes signata* 'Pumila', zinnia.

Sow in mid-spring: tagetes (French, African and Afro-French marigolds), *Tagetes signata* 'Pumila', zinnia.

Sowing techniques as discussed for houseplants in Chapter 23. A temperature of 18–21°C (65–70°F) is required for germination. Seedlings are generally pricked out into seed trays to give them room to grow, approximately 45 seedlings per standard-size seed tray. Some, though, can be pricked out into 9 cm ($3\frac{1}{2}$ in) pots, including centaurea, dahlia and pelargonium. If you want only a few plants there is no reason why all of those listed should not be potted individually – you may find they take up less space than seed trays.

TENDER VEGETABLES FROM SEEDS

These are raised in the same way as summer bedding plants (again I refer you to Chapter

The weeping fig, *Ficus benjamina*, eventually grows quite large, when it makes a fine specimen plant. Light from the window shining through it enhances the effect.

23 for details of sowing). The following are easily raised on a window-sill:

Aubergines Sow in early spring, prick out into 7.5 cm (3 in) pots, and pot on to 12.5 cm (5 in) pots. Pinch out tips when 15 cm (6 in) high.

Beans, French and runner Sow mid-spring, one per 7.5 cm (3 in) pot.

Capsicum (sweet pepper) Sow in early spring, prick out into 7.5 cm (3 in) pots, and pot on to 12.5 cm (5 in) pots. When plants are 15 cm (6 in) high, pinch out tips.

Celery Sow early spring and prick out into a seed tray.

Cucumbers, outdoor Sow mid-spring, two seeds per 9 cm ($3\frac{1}{2}$ in) pot. Remove weakest seedling if both germinate.

Marrows Sow mid-spring as for cucumbers.

Sweet corn Sow mid-spring, one seed per 7.5 cm (3 in) pot.

Tomatoes, outdoor varieties Sow early spring. Prick out into 7.5 cm (3 in) pots, and pot on to 12.5 cm (5 in) pots.

None of these should be placed outside until all danger of frost is over.

STARTING TUBERS INTO GROWTH

Tuberous plants which are used for summer display outdoors can be started off in warmth indoors. Again do not plant out until late spring when all danger of frost is over.

Begonias, tuberous Very popular for summer bedding and for outdoor containers. Start them into growth in late winter to early spring by pressing them into a tray of moist peat (hollow surface uppermost) and providing a temperature of 18°C (65°F). When shoots start to develop pot singly into 12.5 cm (5 in) pots. The top of each tuber should be level with the compost surface. Provide maximum light at all times.

Cannas (Indian shot lilies) These are started into growth in exactly the same way as tuberous begonias, but just cover the fleshy rhizomes with peat.

Dahlias Both dwarf bedding and tall varieties can be grown from tubers, starting them into growth in mid to late spring in the same way as tuberous begonias. Pot into suitably sized pots and ensure maximum light until planting time. Alternatively, dormant tubers can be planted direct in the open in mid to late spring – recommended if you find you lack space indoors for starting them off.

CUTTINGS OF HARDY PLANTS

All kinds of hardy plants can be raised from stem cuttings on a window-sill indoors, ideally in an electrically heated propagating case. The technique of preparing and inserting stem cuttings is the same as for houseplants (see Chapter 23). In the spring many shrubs and herbaceous plants can be raised from soft shoots; while in summer and autumn many more shrubs and conifers are raised from semi-ripe cuttings (the base of the cutting being hard and woody, while the top is still soft and green). Once the cuttings are well-rooted and have been potted individually, they will need to be acclimatized gradually to outdoor conditions.

SEEDS OF HARDY PLANTS

Look through any good seed catalogue and you will find many hardy perennials and shrubs which can be raised from seeds. These can, of course, be sown out of doors, but equally good results are possible on a window-sill in a cool room. You do not really need to use a warm propagating case, unless heat is recommended in the catalogue or on the seed packet. I generally reserve window-sill space for very fine or small seeds, which are more easily sown in pots than in the open ground. When seedlings have been potted and are established they should be acclimatized to outdoor conditions, as hardy plants must not be coddled or they will become weak and spindly.

5
WINTER STORAGE

Tender plants from the garden, balcony, etc., which have been grown for summer display, such as tuberous begonias, cannas, dahlias, fuchsias, gladiolus and pelargoniums, can be stored for the winter indoors. They should not be left outside over winter as frosts will kill them.

BEGONIAS, TUBEROUS

These should be lifted before the frosts, generally in early autumn. At this time it is unlikely the plants will be dying down, so they should be replanted into a box of moist peat. Keep them growing in a warm room indoors, in maximum light, until the foliage starts to turn yellow. This is the signal to start drying off the plants, by gradually reducing watering until eventually the peat is dry.

When the stems are completely dead carefully cut or snap them off the tubers. Then place the tubers in a box of dry peat, completely covering them, and store in a cool room – they need a temperature of 7°C (45°F) for successful storage. Check the tubers occasionally over the winter and if they appear to be shrivelling slightly moisten the peat.

CANNA

If these have been planted out in beds or containers, lift them before the frosts, towards early autumn. Before you remove the old stems and roots, the plants are best partially dried off. When stems and roots are dying back they should be trimmed off. The fleshy rhizomes should then be placed in a box of slightly moist peat and stored in the same conditions as begonias. On no account keep the peat wet or the rhizomes may rot; on the other hand, if it is allowed to become very

dry they may shrivel and the dormant growth buds may die off, so the rhizomes will not start into growth in the spring.

If the plants have been grown in pots, and simply stood outside for the summer, then I would recommend storing them in their pots over the winter, repotting into fresh compost in the spring. The plants should be gradually dried off in the autumn and then the top growth cut down. Remember the compost should not become bone dry in the winter.

DAHLIAS

Dahlias of all kinds (the dwarf bedding varieties and the tall ones) are kept outside until the frosts of autumn blacken their foliage. Then they should be carefully lifted to avoid damaging the tubers, and have their stems cut down to within 15 cm (6 in) of the tubers. Remove any adhering soil and then take the tubers indoors to dry off. Choose a moderately warm, airy room for this – or even an enclosed porch. Dry off the tubers for a couple of weeks or so, by standing them upside down, say in a cardboard box, or in seed trays, as this allows moisture to drain out of the stems. If moisture is left in the stems over the winter there is risk of rot setting in.

When the tubers are thoroughly dry, brush off any dry soil still remaining, and then place them, the right way up, in a suitable container, such as a cardboard box, tomato tray, etc. Store them in the same conditions as tuberous begonias. They need a very airy place as a damp atmosphere can cause rot to set in; so ensure there is good air circulation around the tubers. Do not, for instance, store them in an airless cupboard. Do check the tubers regularly over the winter and if any are showing signs of rotting, cut away the affected

Plants thriving in this light and airy room include the fig, *Ficus carica*, a yucca and, with pink flowers, an oleander.

parts and dust the areas with flowers of sulphur. Do not subject the tubers to high temperatures over the winter, or they will dry out and shrivel.

FUCHSIAS

If tender fuchsias have been grown outside for summer display take them indoors in early autumn. If the plants have been planted out, lift carefully, shake off most of the soil from around the roots, and pot into suitably sized pots, using John Innes potting compost No. 1. Do not be afraid to carry out a little root pruning if some of the roots are too long.

The plants are rested over the winter by gradually reducing watering from mid autumn onwards. This will encourage them to shed their leaves. When the leaves have fallen and throughout the winter keep the compost only barely moist and the plants as cool as possible, but do not allow frost to get at them. An unheated room indoors should be satisfactory. Either soon after leaf-fall, or in early spring, prune back all side shoots to within two or three buds of their base. You may prefer to do this in autumn as the plants will then take up less space indoors over the winter.

In early spring start the plants into growth by increasing the temperature – 10°C (50°F) – and gradually stepping up watering. Provide the plants with maximum light if the young shoots are not to become weak and spindly. Fuchsias can be kept many years but, of course, they will gradually become larger and take up more space.

GLADIOLUS

These grow from corms and are very popular for summer display and for cutting, being planted out in early to mid-spring in a sunny spot in the garden. They can, of course, be grown in large containers on a balcony. The corms are lifted when the leaves start to turn yellow, this generally being in mid-autumn. Certainly lift them before hard frosts com-

mence. Rub off any soil adhering to the corms and cut off the stem about 12 mm ($\frac{1}{2}$ in) above the corm. The corms should be dried off thoroughly; this takes about two weeks in a cool but frost-proof, airy room. It is best to lay them out in trays to dry off so that air can circulate around them.

When dry, clean off the corms – first break off the old shrivelled corm at the base of the new one; remove any small cormlets around the new corm, and rub off any tough loose skin. Then place the cleaned corms in shallow trays, such as seed trays, and store in the same conditions as tuberous begonias. Check the corms regularly over winter, and if any are seen to be rotting remove and discard before they affect healthy corms.

PELARGONIUMS

Widely used for summer bedding and for ornamental containers, they must be lifted before the autumn frosts start, potted into suitable-sized pots, have their stems cut back and overwintered in the same way as tender fuchsias. Keep the compost only slightly moist and ensure maximum light. Zonal and ivy-leaved pelargoniums can be treated in this way.

The difficult period is from early spring, when you start them into growth again by increasing the temperature and watering. Very bright light is needed, as in poor light conditions the new shoots quickly become weak and spindly, resulting in poor plants for setting outside in late spring. They will not flower so well as plants with thick, sturdy, short-jointed shoots.

Over the winter regularly pick off any dead and dying (yellowing) leaves otherwise the plants may become infected with botrytis or grey mould. This will then spread to other leaves and the stems, causing them to rot. If this happens cut away all rotted parts and dust the plants with a fungicide such as flowers of sulphur. An airy atmosphere will do much to prevent grey mould from becoming established.

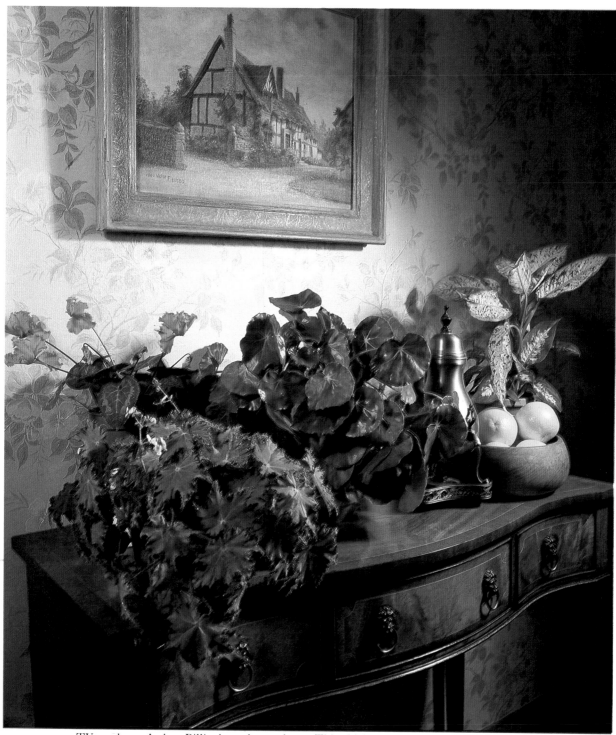

TV gardener Arthur Billitt loves houseplants. This sideboard at his home, Clack's Farm, features some beautiful foliage begonias. Polished wood makes a superb background for plants.

Part 2

GROWING FRUITS AND VEGETABLES INDOORS

6
PRODUCTIVE WINDOW-SILLS

I am not saying that you can have a complete vegetable and fruit 'garden' in the rooms of the house, but at least you can grow some kinds of utility crops if you have some very sunny window-sills, for the secret of successful fruit and vegetable growing indoors is the provision of maximum light. In this respect, enclosed porches may well be suitable, too, for utility crops, as they would perhaps most closely resemble greenhouse conditions, the normal method of growing most of the crops discussed here.

If you grow crops on a window-sill be sure to turn the plants regularly, giving them a quarter turn each time, so that all parts of each plant receive an equal share of good bright light. It should also be said here that artificial lighting is a great boon to indoor vegetable and fruit growing (see Chapter 16).

Tomatoes
Among the most satisfactory candidates for indoor cultivation are the modern dwarf bush varieties like 'Tiny Tim', with 2.5 cm (1 in) diameter fruits; 'Pixie', again with small round fruits; 'Minibel', 30 cm (12 in) high, laden with small fruits; and 'Florida Petit', 15 cm (6 in) high, small-fruited.

Sow seeds in early spring and germinate at 18°C (65°F). Prick out seedlings into 7.5 cm (3 in) pots, pot on to 12.5 cm (5 in) pots and eventually into final 15 cm (6 in) pots. Use soil-based John Innes composts for raising and potting.

Tomatoes like warmth, sunshine and dryish air, so provide the optimum temperature of 15.5–21°C (60–70°F), with a minimum of 13°C (55°F) at night. Keep well watered and start feeding once a week with a proprietary tomato fertilizer once the first fruits start to form. Pollinate the flowers as they open by gently tapping the trusses of flowers daily.

Aubergine
The egg plant is grown in exactly the same way as tomatoes. Choose varieties like 'Short Tom', only 76 cm (2½ ft) high, early and prolific; and 'Easter Egg' with white fruits. When the young plants are 15 cm (6 in) high pinch out the tips to encourage branching and therefore more fruits.

Capsicum
Sweet peppers are also grown in exactly the same way as tomatoes. I can recommend the varieties 'Triton', 25 cm (10 in) high, a true dwarf, and the taller 'Twiggy', with heavy crops of very sweet 'peppers'. When the young plants are 15 cm (6 in) high pinch out the growing tips to encourage branching.

Cucumber
I recommend the all-female flowering F1 hybrids of cucumber, like the small-growing 'Petita' which produces mini-cucumbers, and 'Fembaby'. Sow seeds in early spring, one per 7.5 cm (3 in) pot, using soilless compost. Germinate at 24°C (75°F). Pot on to 12.5 cm (5 in) pots, and eventually into final 15 cm (6 in) pots, again using soilless compost.

Cucumbers like plenty of humidity so spray the leaves daily with plain water. Try to provide a daytime temperature of 18–21°C (65–70°F), with a minimum at night of 15.5°C (60°F). Train the stems up bamboo canes to give them support. Feed weekly with a liquid fertilizer from about six weeks after final potting. Lightly shade from the strongest sun-

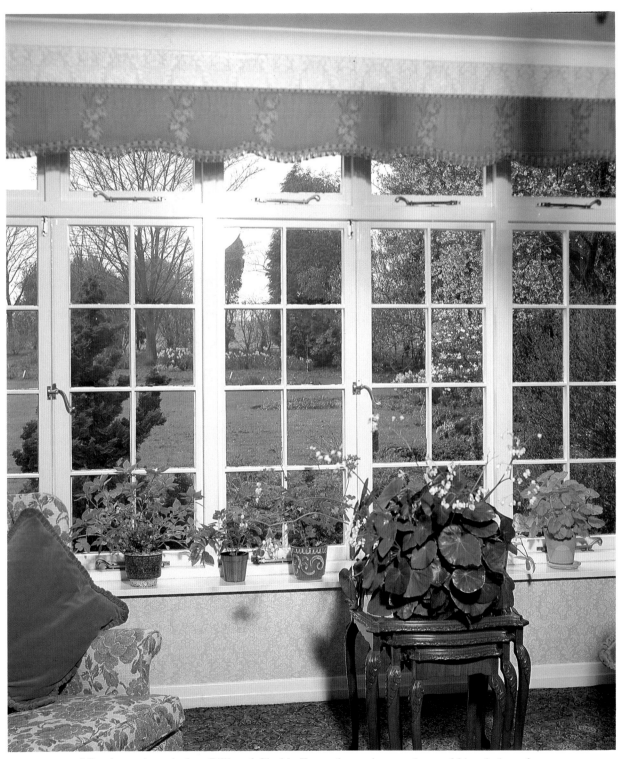

Like the author, Arthur Billitt of Clack's Farm also makes good use of his windows for displaying houseplants. Light shining through the leaves enhances many plants.

shine, and keep the compost steadily moist. Avoid wetting bases of stems, though, as it can result in rotting.

A little training is needed – the tip of the main stem can be pinched out when it reaches a reasonable height; the tendrils should be removed; and the side shoots should be pinched out at two leaves beyond a female flower.

Okra

Ladies fingers (*Hibiscus esculentus*) is becoming rather better-known these days with the great interest in foreign cooking, the pods being used especially in oriental dishes. The plant grows about 1 m (3 ft) high and has attractive pale yellow flowers, followed by the green pods.

Sow seeds in late winter to early spring and germinate at 15.5°C (60°F). Pot on and grow as for tomatoes, providing the plants with a very sunny spot, but shade lightly from really scorching sun. A cane will be needed for support. A good variety is 'Tender Pod', a modern F1 hybrid.

Salad crops

A few salad crops are suitable for cultivation on a very light window-sill, including spring or salad onions. Grow these in pots in a cool room. I like to grow them out of season, in other words, to give supplies of fresh salad onions in the winter. A temperature of 10°C (50°F) is perfectly adequate and sowing can be made, fairly thickly in pots, in early autumn. Keep the compost steadily moist, but not too wet, and ensure airy conditions. Pull when large enough to use. 'White Lisbon' is the usual variety.

I do not find lettuce particularly successful indoors, but instead, for winter salads, I grow a lettuce substitute – corn salad or lamb's lettuce. This tastes like lettuce and is used in the same way, the leaves being picked when three or four have formed, so you do not have long to wait before harvesting. Pick off a few leaves as required – more will follow. Sow seeds between late summer and early autumn. Germinate and grow on in a cool room, but do ensure maximum light. Prick out the seedlings individually into small pots.

Herbs

I like to grow a few herbs indoors for autumn and winter use, a window-sill in a cool room being suitable. Plants of basil, borage, chives, sweet marjoram, mint, sage, summer and winter savory, tarragon and thyme can either be bought pot-grown from a garden centre, or plants from the garden can be lifted and potted in early autumn and taken indoors. Chervil and parsley can be sown in pots in late summer.

Sprouting seeds

Seed sprouting is increasing in popularity and can be done all the year round. However, many people like to produce seed sprouts in autumn and winter when there may be a lack of fresh vegetables.

The technique is simple enough – seeds are sprouted (in other words, germinated) in moist, warm conditions. They are used when the shoots are a few centimetres in length. The nutritious seed sprouts are used in salads, sandwiches etc., and also in Chinese cooking, of course. You do not have to wait long for results, either: harvesting can take place within a matter of days, the exact time depending on temperature. A useful temperature range to provide is 13–21°C (55–70°F). It is important to buy only seeds intended for sprouting – they are available from seedsmen and from health-food shops.

There are two methods of sprouting seeds. The traditional way is in a shallow tray with absorbent material in the bottom, such as layers of tissue paper or flannel. The seeds are sown thickly on this material which is kept moist. They are germinated in normal light.

The second method makes use of a glass jar, such as a large jam jar. The first step is to soak the seeds in water for several hours to plump them up. Then rinse them thoroughly in clean water and place a 12 mm ($\frac{1}{2}$ in) layer of them in the jar. Cover the top of the jar with a piece of muslin, secured with an elastic band. Every morning and evening the seeds should be rinsed with clean water, which is added and drained off again through the muslin. The seeds should be kept in complete darkness to ensure white sprouts (which is what is required with this method). If placed in light the sprouts will be green.

The following are among the popular kinds of seeds for sprouting but there are many others available, including mixtures of several kinds. The appropriate method of sprouting is given for each one.

Adzuki beans Jar method. Sprouts used when 1.8 cm ($\frac{3}{4}$ in) long (four to six days).

Alfalfa Jar method. Sprouts used when 2.5 cm (1 in) long (five to seven days).

Alphatoco beans Jar method. Sprouts used when 1.8 cm ($\frac{3}{4}$ in) long (four to six days).

Cress Very popular. Tray method. Use when 5 cm (2 in) high and seed leaves have appeared (15 to 20 days).

Fenugreek Jar method. Sprouts used when 12 mm ($\frac{1}{2}$ in) long (three to five days).

Lentils Jar method. Use whole lentils. Sprouts used when 1.8 cm ($\frac{3}{4}$ in) long (five to six days).

Mung beans Jar method. Sprouts used when 1.8 cm ($\frac{3}{4}$ in) long (four to six days).

Mustard Very popular – often used with cress. Tray method. Cut when 5 cm (2 in) high and seed leaves have appeared (12 to 15 days).

Rape Tray method. Cut when 5 cm (2 in) high and seed leaves have appeared (12 to 18 days).

Strawberries

These are the most successful fruits for in-door cultivation and they need a really sunny window-sill or porch. As with other plants, turn the pots round regularly so all parts of the plants receive an equal amount of light. They can either be grown in 15 cm (6 in) pots, or in a Tower Pot, a proprietary product consisting of a tall cylinder with planting 'pockets' protruding from the sides. This takes up far less space than numerous pots.

The idea of growing strawberries indoors is to force them, so that they ripen several weeks ahead of outdoor plants. The technique is normally carried out in a heated greenhouse.

Buy young plants in mid-summer and pot them into 12.5 cm (5 in) pots of John Innes potting compost No. 2, or direct into a Tower Pot, using JI P3. They must be stood in the open until mid winter – on a balcony if you do not have a garden. Then pot into 15 cm (6 in) pots, using JI P3, and take indoors, placing them in maximum light. To start with a temperature of around 4.5°C (40°F) is adequate, but by the time the plants are in flower (generally mid-spring), they should be in a temperature of 15.5°C (60°F). The flowers must be hand pollinated by dabbing the centre of each in turn with a soft artist's brush. From the time the flowers start to open give a liquid feed every 10 days. Do not force the plants again, but they can be planted outdoors. Recommended varieties are 'Cambridge Vigour', 'Red Gauntlet' and 'Rival'.

7
CELLARS AND CUPBOARDS

Cellars, cupboards and utility areas can all be put to good use for indoor gardening, such as storing crops for winter use and for forcing vegetables.

MUSHROOMS

These can be grown in utility areas – they do not need to be grown in the dark as many people imagine, although commercial producers do in fact grow them in completely dark 'mushroom houses' or sheds.

There has been a quiet revolution in home mushroom growing in recent years with the introduction of mushroom kits (Fig. 2), which are bought either in plastic tubs or in strong cardboard boxes, in which the mushrooms are grown. These make mushroom growing in the home very easy and foolproof.

The tub or box is bought ready filled with special compost which has been 'sown' with the correct quantity of mushroom 'spawn'. Also provided is the 'casing' or top-dressing material which is spread over the compost as indicated in the instructions. All you have to do is water the compost and place the kit anywhere indoors in a temperature of 13–18°C (55–65°F), but avoid direct sunlight.

One can expect the first mushrooms to be ready in about four weeks or so and then cropping should continue for approximately another eight weeks. Full instructions are supplied with these kits and, of course, for best results these should be followed to the letter.

Mushroom kits are available from some of the leading seedsmen in the UK and also from garden centres.

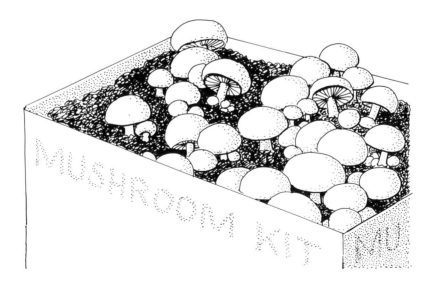

Fig. 2. Mushroom growing in the home is easy and foolproof if a proprietary kit is used. Picking can extend over at least two months.

RHUBARB

Rhubarb can be forced indoors for early or out-of-season crops, particularly if you do not have a heated greenhouse, which is the normal place for this method of production. Darkness is needed, so a cupboard or cellar may be the ideal places in your home.

If you have some large crowns or plants in the garden, dig up a few in the autumn when the leaves have died down and lay them on the ground for a couple of weeks to subject them to frosts. It is unlikely you will be able to buy large crowns, although you may be able to beg some from a gardening friend if you do not have a garden.

Plant the crowns in a deep wooden box, using sandy soil or compost, and making sure the dormant buds are showing above the surface of the compost. Water well in, allow to drain off, and then place in a dark place, with a temperature of 7–15.5°C (45–60°F). Keep the compost steadily moist, but not wet.

Of course, the higher the temperature you are able to maintain the quicker the stems will be produced. They should be ready for harvesting in approximately five to eight weeks. After harvesting the stems the roots are discarded as they are not suitable for forcing again; or plant them out in the garden.

CHICORY

If you have grown some chicory in the garden the roots should be lifted from mid-autumn onwards in succession and forced as for rhubarb, in a temperature of 7–10°C (45–50°F).

The parsnip-like roots can have their bottoms trimmed if they are too long, and the leaves should be cut off close to the top of the root. The roots are planted vertically in a deep box of sandy soil or compost, ensuring the tops of the roots are level with the compost surface. Water in and then cover with a 10-cm (8-in) layer of moist peat. Place in a completely dark place.

Within four to six weeks blanched (white)

shoots should have been produced, known as 'chicons', which are cut and used for winter salads, etc. The chicons should be cut when 15 cm (6 in) high, before the leaves unfold. After harvesting, the roots are discarded. Good varieties, which are raised from seeds sown outdoors in spring, are 'Normato' and 'Witloof'.

STORING ROOT VEGETABLES

If you do not have a frost-free outbuilding, such as a shed or garage, root vegetables can be stored indoors for winter use (maincrop varieties of root vegetables which have been grown in the open). For instance, you may be able to store them in a cellar, utility area or cupboard. Cool but frost-free conditions are recommended.

Rootcrops like carrots, beetroots, parsnips, swedes and turnips are lifted in autumn and placed between layers of slightly moist sand or peat in deep wooden boxes or other suitable containers. Start off with a layer of sand/peat in the bottom, add a layer of roots, cover with sand/peat, add another layer of roots, and so on until the box is filled, and then top off with a layer of sand/peat. Remember to cut off the leaves before storing; or, in the case of beetroots, twist them off.

Maincrop potatoes are best dried off before storing in paper sacks. Keep them completely dark or they will turn green and be unfit for eating. Onions should be thoroughly dried off before being stored in a cool dry place. The best method is to tie them, by their withered leaves, on to a piece of rope, and to hang them up.

Regularly check vegetables in store and remove any which may be showing signs of rotting. To help guard against this, avoid storing any vegetables which are damaged.

STORING FRUITS

Apples and pears can also be stored indoors if you do not have a frost-proof outbuilding. Mid-season and late varieties are the ones to store, but keep the two kinds apart; in other words, do not store them together in the same place.

A good place for fruit storage is a cool cellar, utility area or even an attic, provided it does not become too warm. The ideal storage temperature is 4–7°C (40–45°F). Conditions must be airy, too. A slightly moist atmosphere is also recommended, but this may not be feasible indoors. Just bear in mind that if the air is very dry the fruits may shrivel.

Fruits are conveniently stored in shallow tomato trays with corner posts, which can be stacked. But any flat tray would be suitable. I like to lay a sheet of thin polythene over the fruits to help prevent them from shrivelling.

Store only undamaged fruits. Pears are simply placed in a single layer in the trays. Apples can be wrapped individually with newspaper before placing them in several layers in the trays.

An alternative way of storing apples and pears is in clear polythene bags, particularly recommended if you are storing in a very dry atmosphere. Each bag should contain no more than 2.2 kg (5 lb) of fruit. Before placing the fruits in the bags allow them to cool off, otherwise a lot of condensation will occur in the bags. Do not make the bag completely airtight – simply fold over the top and make a few small holes in it – approximately two for each 454 g (1 lb) of fruit.

All fruits should be checked regularly and any showing signs of rotting removed immediately. Mid-season varieties can generally be stored for four to eight weeks, but late varieties will keep for between three and six months, depending on the particular variety.

Of course, now that many households are equipped with a deep-freeze cabinet the above methods may be considered obsolete by many people. Most fruits can be stored well by freezing, with the exception of strawberries and dessert varieties of pears. For freezing techniques I refer you to a book on the subject.

Part 3

DISPLAYING
HOUSEPLANTS

8

BUYING HOUSEPLANTS

Houseplants can be bought from several sources, probably the most popular being local garden centres and florists. Many of these stock a very wide range of plants and apart from well-known popular kinds, several of the more unusual plants are obtainable. Indeed, each year sees a sprinkling of houseplants that have not before been available.

In the UK there are several mail-order suppliers of houseplants from whom it is possible to obtain a wider selection of the more unusual species and varieties. They generally advertise in the gardening press and some exhibit at flower shows throughout the country, where orders can often be placed.

There are, too, specialist suppliers offering a mail-order service. For instance, in the UK there are nurserymen specializing in bromeliads, cacti and succulents, pelargoniums, fuchsias, saintpaulias (African violets), ferns, and the like.

HOW TO ENSURE QUALITY PLANTS

If you buy from garden centres, florists and chain stores, you should inspect plants closely before you buy to ensure they are of good quality. The following tips will help.
● As a general observation, plants should, of course, look in the peak of health.
● Check the foliage carefully – it should not have any brown marks or patches, nor brown or dried up margins.
● The leaves should not be showing signs of wilting.
● Green-leaved plants should be a good shade of green and not look pale and insipid, while coloured-foliage plants should be showing good bright colours.

● The compost should be moist. If it is dry there is a possibility that leaves and flower buds may drop when you get the plant home.
● Plants should be well-established in their pots – not loose, which indicates they have only recently been potted.
● If you are buying flowering plants there should be several flowers fully open, with plenty of buds yet to open.
● It goes almost without saying that plants should be free from pests and diseases. Check closely leaves and stems, including shoot tips, to make sure there are no pests like aphids, scale insects or mealy bugs. Very fine pale mottling on leaves is an indication of red-spider mites. White patches on leaves could well be mildew, while a grey mould on flowers, buds or leaves is almost certainly botrytis disease.
● Make sure the display area is suitably warm for if plants are kept in a cold, draughty place you could have problems when you get them home – such as leaf- and flower-bud drop. The plants may even die if they have been kept in cold draughty conditions. With this in mind, never buy houseplants which are displayed out of doors, such as on a pavement in front of a shop, or open market stall.

Having given some guidelines on plant quality, I feel we must be fair to suppliers, for the majority of garden centres, florists and so on look after their plants carefully while they are waiting to be sold, keeping them in suitably warm conditions and carrying out regular care such as watering.

WHEN TO BUY PLANTS

Houseplants can be bought at any time of

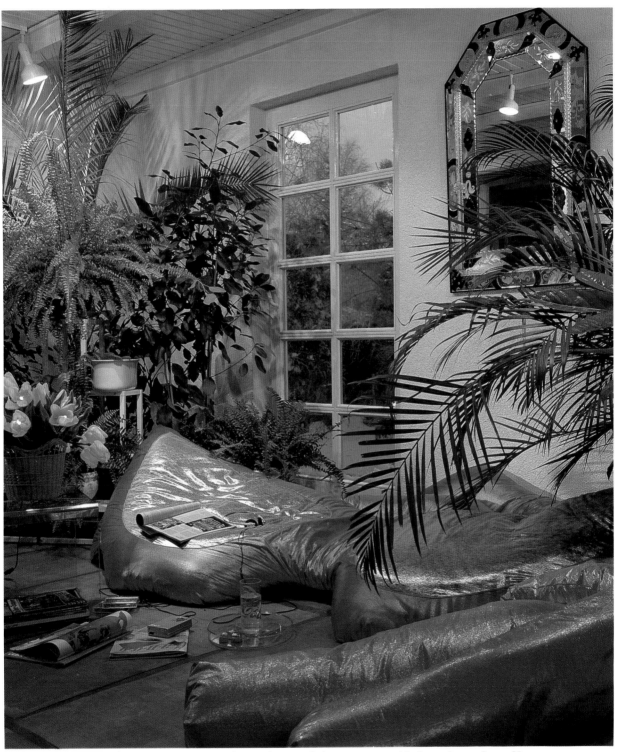

Palms are very popular as specimen plants and there are many kinds to choose from. Here ferns are also being used to create a lush 'jungle' effect.

year but it is sensible to try to buy them when the weather is warm, say in early summer, so that they have the summer in front of them in which to settle down and gradually become acclimatized to winter conditions, when the light is poorer and temperatures may be lower than in the greenhouses on the nursery where they were raised.

Most houseplants dislike sudden changes in growing conditions and may react by dropping leaves, wilting or even dying in the case of very delicate plants.

You should bear in mind that the plants are raised in optimum conditions in the nursery greenhouses: they are given sufficient warmth and humidity, and the correct light levels — very different from rooms in your home. So the plants must, if possible, be gradually acclimatized to your home. This is most easily achieved, as already mentioned, in the summer.

Flowering pot-plants are bought at the appropriate season, though. Fortunately, many of the popular kinds need cool conditions, anyway, so we do not have the problem of acclimatization.

When buying plants from a garden centre, florist, chain store, and the like, do ensure they are well wrapped before you take them out of the shop as this will protect them from cold conditions, draughts, etc, on the journey home.

If you are transporting plants by car, do remember that cars can become extremely hot inside during warm weather and in these conditions also plants will suffer. Try, therefore, not to leave plants in the car for longer than absolutely necessary. If left in a car boot for several hours on a hot day they could be severely scorched and damaged.

9

SPECIMEN PLANTS

Many houseplants lend themselves to being grown in isolation, as specimen plants to act as focal points, or to create a dramatic room feature. Generally large plants are used: those with large bold foliage or with a particularly distinctive shape or habit of growth. Smaller plants, too, can be used as single specimens provided they have some distinctive feature.

It must be admitted that the British are not too adventurous when it comes to specimen plants: the usual choice is *Ficus elastica*, the rubber plant; *Monstera deliciosa*, the Swiss cheese plant; and, perhaps, as a smaller specimen, *Sansevieria trifasciata* 'Laurentii', the mother-in-law's tongue. However, there is a very wide range of suitable candidates, as our friends in the USA will testify. The descriptive list later in this chapter should hopefully inspire people to be more adventurous.

The pots of specimen plants should be placed in pot holders of some kind, for ordinary growing pots do nothing to add to the beauty of plants. Be careful in your choice of ornamental pot-holders, though, for they should not detract from the beauty of the plant, and certainly should not be dominant. I prefer to use containers in natural or pastel colours, such as shades of buff, beige, cream, pale brown and greens. I generally avoid patterned containers as I find the eye immediately latches on to these rather than the plants. Pot holders are generally cylindrical, but I am always on the lookout for square ones – for some reason, which I honestly cannot explain, they seem to look more stylish.

Specimen plants can be positioned in many parts of a room. Large plants obviously stand on the floor, and can be placed in corners, alcoves, alongside a coffee table, at the side or just behind a chair or settee, in a fireplace, and so on, always provided there is sufficient light for the health of the plant. Spotlights can, of course, be used to illuminate specimen plants, particularly if they are in a shady part of the room. In the hours of darkness such lighting can create a really dramatic effect.

Smaller specimen plants are ideal for table centrepieces or for displaying on some other piece of furniture. They can even be placed in a plant stand or jardinière.

A SELECTION OF PLANTS

Abutilon striatum 'Thompsonii'
Although not generally thought of as a houseplant, this large shrub makes a superb specimen if you can provide light airy conditions for it. The large maple-like leaves are heavily splashed and mottled with yellow. It needs only average warmth and in winter should be kept cool, at around 10°C (50°F). Water and feed well in summer and prune hard back in early spring to ensure bushy rather than leggy growth. It can be placed outdoors or in a porch in summer if desired.

Alocasia amazonica
Not too easy to find, but the easiest of the genus to grow indoors, this is a marvellous foliage plant with large, broad, arrow-shaped leaves, deep green, with the veins conspicuously picked out in white. It grows from fleshy rhizomes and is best in a peat-based compost. Provide bright light but avoid direct sun. Very warm conditions are needed, with high humidity, but in the winter rest the

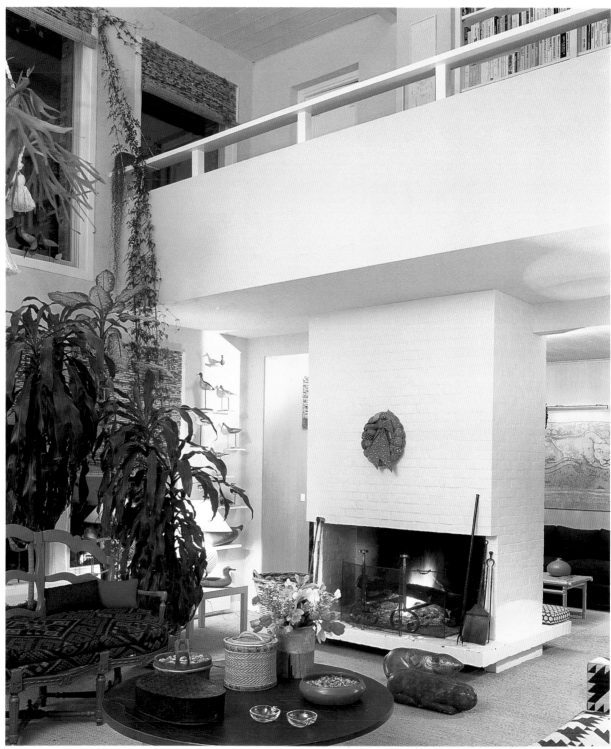

An example of how an ultra-modern room can be decorated with plants, including trailing kinds cascading over a balcony. Being green foliage plants they create a restful effect.

plant at about 15.5°C (60°F) and water more sparingly. A suitable plant for a warm steamy bathroom or kitchen, perhaps?

Anthurium crystallinum

This needs the same conditions as alocasia, and like that plant has dramatic foliage – broad velvety leaves up to 60 cm (24 in) long, deep green, with the veins picked out in silvery white. Until recently this species was difficult to obtain but there is at least one houseplant company in the UK who can now supply it. As with alocasia, do ensure, before you buy, that you can provide the warmth and humidity that it needs.

Beaucarnea recurvata (PONY TAIL)

This, like the anthurium, is another plant that has only recently become available, although it is easier to obtain, for it can be found in garden centres and chain stores. It is related to the yucca and the base of the stem is curiously swollen. It is bought as a small plant, suitable for the table, but eventually it can form a trunk and become quite tall. It carries a rosette of thin arching grassy leaves which are deepish green. As it is able to store water, watering should be moderate at all times, and it will tolerate a dry atmosphere. Normal living-room temperature is suitable, but do not subject the plant to a temperature lower than 10°C (50°F). It likes bright light, including some sunshine.

Chamaedorea erumpens (BAMBOO PALM)

Perhaps not as well-known in Britain as in the USA, this palm is extremely durable, being shade-loving and suited to air-conditioned buildings. It produces cane-like stems – up to at least 1.8 m (6 ft) when the plant is happy – these carrying deep green pinnate fronds right down to the base. Do not overpot – pot on only when the present pot is packed full of roots. Water only when the compost is drying out. Ordinary living-room temperatures are suitable, but not below 10°C (50°F). Provide high humidity in warm conditions.

Chamaerops humilis (EUROPEAN FAN PALM)

This is one of the easiest of the fan palms, the segments, which form the fronds, radiating like a fan from the top of the leaf stalk. It generally remains quite dwarf so is suitable for the average-sized room. It thrives in similar conditions to chamaedorea but will take much lower temperatures and is ideal for cool rooms.

Cycas revoluta (SAGO PALM)

Not a true palm, but it looks like one. A very slow grower – one cannot expect a height of much more than about 60 cm (24 in), so an ideal 'conversation piece' for a table, perhaps. It forms a rosette of stiff, glossy, dark green fronds. It is suitable for a cool room, and indeed prefers cool conditions in winter. Grow in a soil-based compost and do not overpot. Water only when the compost is starting to become dry, far less in cool winter conditions. Provide good bright light but not direct sun.

Dizygotheca elegantissima (FALSE ARALIA)

Prized for its coppery to almost black, thin finger-like leaves, this plant has a very delicate appearance. A slow grower, but it can eventually reach a height of 1.5 m (5 ft) with a spread of 90 cm (3 ft). It is not one of the easiest plants to manage, unfortunately. It needs bright light but not direct sun; draught-free conditions; a temperature during the day of at least 18°C (65°F), a minimum of 13°C (55°F) at night; and high humidity. Water only when the compost has partially dried out.

Dracaena draco (DRAGON TREE)

The various kinds of dracaena are used as specimen plants, and very dramatic they can be when they attain a reasonable size. But this species seems to be somewhat neglected in the home. In the wild it attains a great height, but one should not expect more than 1.2 m (4 ft) or so when grown in room conditions. This plant has a rosette of thick fleshy blue-grey sword-like leaves up to 60 cm (24 in) long. Eventually it forms a thick trunk. It is one of the easiest dracaenas to grow, thriving in a cool room and shade, although bright light is preferred. Water well in the growing season but very sparingly in winter. Best in soil-based compost; pot on only when pot-bound. Provide humidity in warm conditions.

Ficus (FIGS)

The ubiquitous rubber plant, *Ficus elastica*, cannot be dismissed as a specimen plant, but in my opinion there are more attractive species of ficus, like *F. lyrata*, the fiddleback fig, with huge violin-shaped leaves. It is a vigorous grower, soon reaching the ceiling, but before this happens the top can be removed and it will then branch out. I am also fond of *F. benjamina*, the weeping fig, with small shiny oval leaves and an arching habit of growth. It will easily reach a height of 1.8 m (6 ft) and often grows taller. The plant branches naturally and can become quite wide, so is an ideal choice for a spacious room.

Pot on ficus in spring each year for steady growth. Bright light is preferred, but the plants will thrive in shade. Normal living-room temperatures are suitable but the plants should not be subjected to temperatures lower than 15.5°C (60°F). A humid atmosphere is advised; the compost should be kept steadily moist during the growing season, but in winter water only when it is drying out.

Heptapleurum arboricola 'Variegata' (PARASOL PLANT)

This is a striking plant with compound finger-like leaves which are heavily splashed with yellow. Better known is the species itself with plain green foliage. It will reach a height of about 1.8 m (6 ft). Heptapleurums need the steady warmth of a living room and the minimum temperature should be 15.5°C (60°F). Provide high humidity, bright light, water well in the growing period, sparingly in winter, and pot on each spring.

Howea forsteriana (THATCH PALM)

A favourite palm in Britain, easy to care for and growing slowly to a height of about 2.4 m (8 ft) with a spread of 1.8 m (6 ft). The leaflets have an attractive drooping habit. Pot on only when pot-bound, using loam-based compost; keep free from draughts; place in bright light or shade; ensure a minimum temperature of 13°C (55°F); provide a humid atmosphere; and keep the compost moist all year round.

Neoregelia carolinae 'Tricolor'

Many of the bromeliads make superb specimen plants and it is difficult to pick out one from the dozens available. But they do not come much more colourful than *Neoregelia carolinae* 'Tricolor'. It forms a water-holding rosette of arching leaves, well over 30 cm (12 in) long, striped cream, green and pink. At flowering time the centre of the plant becomes bright pink and remains this colour for many months. A superb plant for the table and easy to grow. Normal living-room conditions are suitable, with a minimum temperature of 10°C (50°F). It likes plenty of warmth in the growing season and high humidity. Provide bright light and even a little sun. Water very sparingly in winter, but keep moist in the growing season and the centre filled with fresh water.

Philodendron

Most of the philodendrons make excellent specimen plants, with their bold leaves in a diversity of shapes. Some have a bushy, wide-spreading habit, while other are climbers, best trained up a moss pole. As with bromeliads, it is difficult to pick out just one or two from the wide range available, and one generally ends up recommending one's favourites. In my case these are *Philodendron angustisectum*, a climber with long, deeply dissected dark green leaves, about 1.5 m (5 ft) in height; *P. melanochrysum*, with velvety, blackish green foliage, a climber, not as adaptable as the others; and *P. selloum*, a large bushy species with broad, much-divided, deep green leaves – needs plenty of space.

Plants can be chosen to match a colour scheme of a room. Here pink begonias and saintpaulias or African violets are a good choice.

47

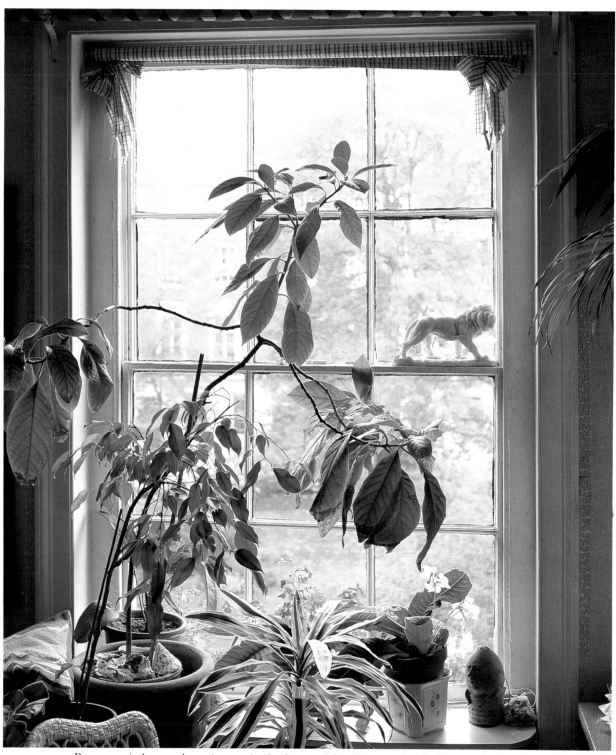

Regency windows make an impressive background for this avocado (the largest plant) and a *Ficus benjamina* or weeping fig.

48

Grow philodendrons in a warm room with a minimum temperature of 15.5°C (60°F), provide high humidity, and water well in the growing season, sparingly in winter. Philodendrons tolerate light shade, and can be placed in areas of poor light, especially if artificial lighting is available.

Phoenix canariensis (CANARY ISLAND DATE PALM)

A popular palm, attaining indoors a height and spread of about 1.2 m (4 ft), with stiff, rather prickly fronds consisting of many thin segments. It tolerates cool conditions and makes a good porch plant. Water sparingly in winter, and pot on only when pot-bound. Ideal plant for light shade.

Strelitzia reginae (BIRD OF PARADISE FLOWER)

You may think this an odd choice but I am very fond of this plant with its large, banana-like leaves. When flowers are produced it is spectacular, as they are orange and blue and shaped like a bird's head. Young plants, though, will not produce flowers. It is easy to grow, overwintering at about 7°C (45°F),

needing very bright light, including plenty of sun, and airy conditions. I place my plant outside for the summer. Water and feed well in the growing season, but be very sparing with water in winter. Height is about 1.5 m (5 ft). It makes a good porch plant, too, and is ideal for a sun room.

Vriesia fenestralis

Another bromeliad – see neoregelia for cultural details. This is also a rosette bromeliad, whose leaves form a water-holding vase. It is a really stylish plant, with light green foliage finely netted and lined with deeper green.

Yucca elephantipes

This plant has become very popular in recent years. The thick trunk carries a rosette of green, erect sword-like leaves. Suitable for cool or warm rooms and dry air, and needing bright light, this is an easy-going plant, especially suitable for porches and sun rooms. Allow compost to partially dry out between waterings, and be very sparing with water in winter. Grow in a clay pot for stability, with soil-based compost.

10
GROUPING HOUSEPLANTS

Houseplant displays should ideally consist not only of large specimen plants, as discussed in Chapter 9, but also groups of plants – a number of different kinds, both flowering and foliage plants, pleasingly arranged to contrast in colour, shape and texture. Even foliage plants alone can create dramatic and colourful effects – there are plants with large hand-shaped leaves, some with sword-like or grassy foliage, and yet others with rounded or heart-shaped leaves. The foliage of many plants is plain green; highly coloured in others; some have glossy leaves while others are hairy or woolly. Combine all these different shapes, textures and colours and you will create some beautiful groups.

There are flowering houseplants for every season, so at no time in the year need a group lack flower colour, but be sparing with flowering plants: use only a few in a group for 'spots' or 'splashes' of colour among foliage plants. A group consisting of a mass of brightly coloured flowers is not exactly restful in a room, even though it is acceptable in the garden (for example, mass planting of summer bedding plants).

WHERE TO ARRANGE GROUPS
Groups of houseplants can be arranged both on the floor and on tables, other pieces of furniture and on window-sills. Generally, larger, bolder plants are used for floor displays, reserving the smaller plants for tables, window-sills, etc.

As with specimen plants, groups can be used to create focal points in a room. For instance, a popular place for a group is in a fireplace. Provided there is sufficient light, also arrange groups in corners, in alcoves and

perhaps alongside pieces of especially attractive furniture: plants contrast beautifully with wood.

Apart from sufficient light, an important consideration is the background. If they are to show up well houseplants need plain backgrounds, such as pastel-coloured walls, or wall coverings such as hessian. If plants are arranged against heavily patterned wallpaper they will simply merge into the background.

Wood panelling makes a superb background for plants, as do large mirrors or mirror tiles. Mirrors give the effect of twice as many plants and, of course, they also reflect light, which is beneficial to the plants.

Generally windows make good backgrounds as the plants will be illuminated from behind. Plants with thin coloured leaves can be very much enhanced with light shining though them as it highlights the colours.

DECORATIVE CONTAINERS
The plants are arranged in decorative containers, of which there is a wide range available from garden centres, in various materials such as plastic and wood. Large containers, intended for floor displays, may be square, rectangular or round, and are generally referred to as 'planters'.

Do not dismiss some of the containers intended for outdoor use, for they can look most attractive in a room setting. Bear in mind, though, that some may be very heavy, particularly those made from concrete, and they may put undue stress on floorboards, although there would be no problem with concrete floors. If you do use outdoor containers you will have to seal or block up the drainage holes in the base. I think that some

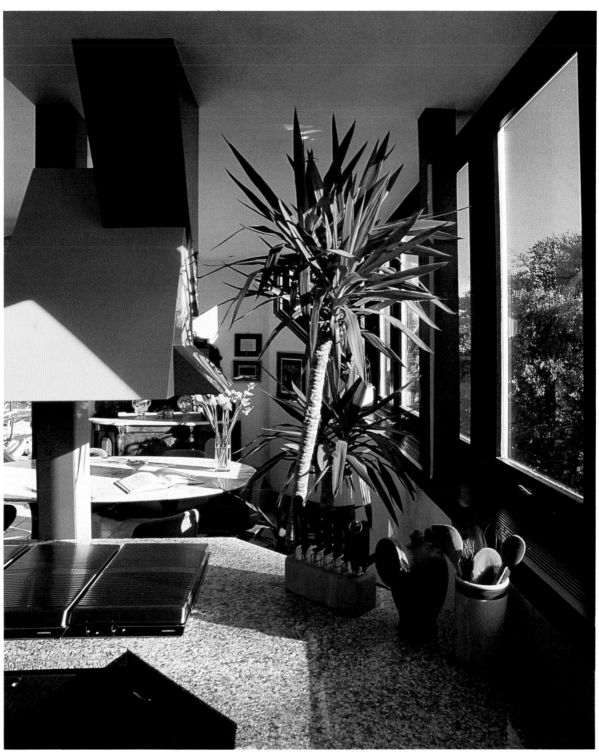

Yuccas are currently very popular as specimen plants and eventually they become quite large. Being 'architectural' plants they are an ideal choice for very modern settings.

of the imitation-stone garden containers can very much enhance a plant display indoors.

Smaller containers are available for tables, window-sills, etc. The trough types are ideal for narrow window-sills.

Containers can be used singly or placed in groups. For instance, on the floor a group of perhaps three square or rectangular planters can look most impressive, and will give you ample space and scope for arranging plants.

They should be placed fairly close together – not widely spaced. Indeed, square or rectangular containers can be butted up against each other. The containers could also vary in height – perhaps having a tall one at the back with lower ones at the front, so that plants can be arranged at various heights.

Houseplants should not be removed from their pots and planted in the containers, for although they will grow exceedingly well

Fig. 3. An attractive way of arranging plants, starting with tall ones at one end of the container, and gradually tapering down to small plants and trailers towards the other end. The plants used here are (*right to left*): dracaena, dieffenbachia, *Ficus pumila*, *Ficus benjamina*, *Begonia* 'Elatior' hybrid, sansevieria, saintpaulia, *Begonia* 'Elatior' hybrid, and *Asparagus densiflorus* 'Sprengeri'.

their roots will become entangled, and therefore it will be extremely difficult to re-arrange the groups at a later date. It is far better to fill the planters with peat and to plunge the pots to their rims in this. If you are using plants which need a humid atmosphere, the peat should be kept moist. As an alternative to peat use one of the lightweight, water-absorbing horticultural aggregates.

ARRANGING PLANTS

When arranging plants in groups aim for some sort of overall shape. For instance, if you want to stage a group in front of a wall, you could arrange them in a triangular shape, achieved by starting with tall plants in the centre, grading down to smaller plants towards the sides and front. Trailing plants could also be used at the sides and front. Alternatively you could start with tall plants at one side, gradually tapering down to small plants and trailers towards the other side (Fig. 3).

If a group is to be viewed from all sides then aim for a pyramid shape. Again start with tall plants in the middle and grade down to shorter plants and trailers towards the edges.

It need not be difficult arranging plants on a narrow window-sill. Use a trough-type container and arrange the plants as I described above for groups against walls. At all costs avoid lining up plants of similar height in a straight row along the windowsill, as is so often seen. This is the least imaginative way of displaying plants.

CONSIDER THE NEEDS OF PLANTS

Successful groups are only achieved if room conditions are suitable for all the plants. All plants in a group must have the same needs in respect of light, temperature and humidity, yet all too often we see unsuitable combinations, such as tropical plants mixed with those which need to be grown in cool rooms,

and plants which need high humidity arranged with subjects that require dry air.

There are sufficient houseplants available to enable you to arrange groups in all kinds of conditions, from cool to warm rooms, from dark corners to bright sunny window-sills. Humidity, if needed, can be provided 'locally', either by keeping the plunging medium (peat or horticultural aggregate) moist, or by spraying the leaves of plants with water.

Throughout this book I have given the basic needs of all plants mentioned so it should be an easy task to group plants accordingly.

SUGGESTIONS FOR GROUPS

Grouping houseplants is very much an artistic exercise – some people have a flare for it, others do not. The possible combinations of plants is almost limitless. It is no wonder, therefore, that some people shy away from grouping plants, leaving it to the professional indoor landscapers in hotels, civic buildings and the like.

Therefore, to help you create some pleasing groups in your home I will put forward some suggestions. These are groups that I have tried out at various times, so I know they work.

Groups for warm rooms
These groups need to be arranged in warm living rooms, with a minimum temperature of 13–15.5°C (55–60°F). All of the plants need high humidity and good bright light, but not direct sunshine.

● A group for winter colour can have as a centrepiece *Euphorbia pulcherrima* or poinsettia, with brilliant scarlet or red bracts (Fig. 4). This is a temporary pot plant, discarded after flowering, but is very popular around Christmas time. To give height at the back or in the centre I suggest a specimen of *Dizygotheca elegantissima* (false aralia), with coppery foliage which blends well with the euphorbia. At the front of the group we need

Fig. 4. A group for winter colour in a warm room, containing (*from back to front*): *Dizygotheca elegantissima, Euphorbia pulcherrima, Vriesia splendens,* and *Ficus pumila.*

some fresh green foliage and I suggest the trailing fig, *Ficus pumila*, a very popular houseplant. For further contrast in foliage shape and colour I can recommend a plant of *Vriesia splendens*, a rosette bromeliad with bronze and green banded leaves.

● A group for summer colour could have as a centrepiece a plant of *Hibiscus rosa-sinensis*, with red flowers over a very long period (Fig. 5). Suitable foliage plants include *Codiaeum*

variegatum pictum, or croton, with multi-coloured leaves. Choose a plant that has a lot of red in its leaves, and buy a tall specimen to give height to the group. Contrasting well with this and the hibiscus would be *Calathea lancifolia*, with long leaves patterned in deep and emerald-green. For the front of the group a low plant – *Maranta leuconeura* 'Kerchoveana', with rounded greyish green leaves spotted reddish brown.

Fig. 5. A group for summer colour in a warm room, containing (*from back to front*): *Codiaeum variegatum pictum, Calathea lancifolia, Hibiscus rosa-sinensis,* and *Maranta leuconeura* 'Kerchoveana'.

● For spring/early summer try the white, sweetly scented climber, *Stephanotis floribunda*, using it as a centrepiece. Back this with a large plant of *Cordyline terminalis*, with lanceolate, bronze and red leaves. To contrast with this I suggest *Dieffenbachia maculata*, with broad leaves, deep green blotched with white. At the front of the group use *Scindapsus aureus* as a trailer. This is the devil's ivy, a popular plant with green and yellow leaves.

● A group for summer colour – use several plants of impatiens with red or pink flowers. The New Guinea hybrids are especially at-tractive as they have colourful foliage. Impatiens, or busy lizzies, will flower throughout summer. Height and bold foliage could be provided with a Swiss cheese plant (*Monstera deliciosa*), and I would also include a *Cordyline terminalis* (see above). At the front or edge of the group I suggest some plants of *Begonia rex* with multicoloured foliage, and *Scindapsus aureus* (see above).

Groups for cool rooms

These groups should be arranged in cool rooms like entrance halls, landings, and perhaps dining rooms and bedrooms. A temper-

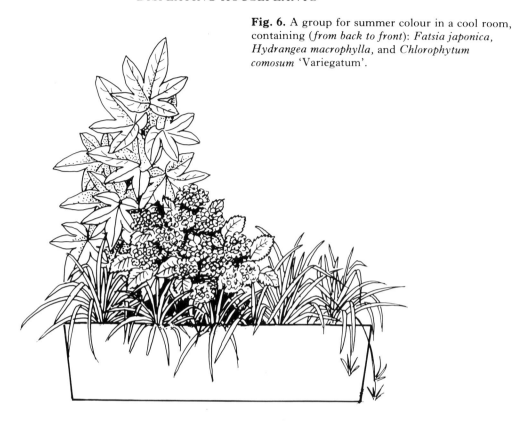

Fig. 6. A group for summer colour in a cool room, containing (*from back to front*): *Fatsia japonica,* *Hydrangea macrophylla,* and *Chlorophytum comosum* 'Variegatum'.

ature range of 7–13°C (45–55°F) would be suitable. The plants will thrive with low humidity.

● A spring group could consist of several plants of *Primula obconica* in pink or red. These are very popular short-term pot plants, being discarded after flowering. We need some nice green ferny or lacy foliage to go with these, such as the silk oak (*Grevillea robusta*). At the edge or front of the group arrange some green or variegated ivies, varieties of *Hedera helix*.

● A summer group could have as a centre-piece a blue pot hydrangea, a variety of *Hydrangea macrophylla* (Fig. 6). This will flower for a very long time and is generally discarded after flowering. We need some large, bold foliage to go with this, so I would suggest a tall specimen of *Fatsia japonica*. This can be used to give height, too. For variation in foliage shape I can recommend, for the edges or front of the group, some

plants of *Chlorophytum comosum* 'Variegatum', the spider plant, with arching grassy leaves striped green and white.

● There are plenty of flowering pot plants for autumn and winter, like cyclamen and *Rhododendron simsii*, the so-called Indian azalea (Fig. 7). These would make a colourful centre-piece for a group, with pink or red flowered varieties. Plenty of green ferny foliage is needed as a foil and could include a tall plant of *Asparagus setaceus* to give height, while at the edges or near the front of the group could be arranged *Asparagus densiflorus* 'Sprengeri'. For contrast in foliage include *Chlorophytum comosum* 'Variegatum' (see above).

I could go on to suggest many more groups, but these will, hopefully, get you started and will certainly ensure colour and interest throughout the year. All of the plants are readily available from garden centres, florists, etc.

56

This Wedgwood vase makes an attractive pot holder for an African violet or saintpaulia. It does not detract from the beauty of the plant.

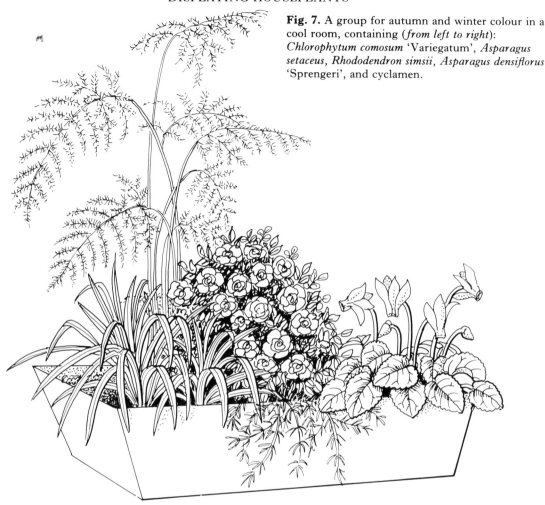

Fig. 7. A group for autumn and winter colour in a cool room, containing (*from left to right*): *Chlorophytum comosum* 'Variegatum', *Asparagus setaceus*, *Rhododendron simsii*, *Asparagus densiflorus* 'Sprengeri', and cyclamen.

Using one type of plant

Some interesting groups can be created by using species and/or varieties of just one type or genera of plant. For instance, a group of begonias can be most attractive, using foliage and flowering kinds like *B. masoniana*, *B. rex*, *B. boweri*, *B.* 'Cleopatra', *B. metallica*, *B. maculata*, *B.* 'Tiger', *B. corallina*, *B.* 'Elatior' hybrids and B. 'Gloire de Lorraine' hybrids. Group these in good light (but avoid direct sun), in a warm room and ensure high humidity.

Bromeliads are ideal for grouping on their own, this time using several genera, as they are so diverse in habit and colour. A bromeliad group would be best in a warm room and the plants need very high humidity. Good bright light is recommended but not direct sun. There are many bromeliads to choose from, some of the most popular being *Aechmea fasciata*, *Ananas comosus* 'Variegatus', *Billbergia horrida*, *B. nutans*, *Cryptanthus bromelioides* 'Tricolor', *C. zonatus*, *Guzmania lingulata*, *Neoregelia carolinae* 'Tricolor', *Nidularium fulgens*, *N. innocentii*, *Vriesia fenestralis* and *V. splendens*.

Ferns of different genera are ideal for grouping together in a shady spot. Most like high humidity and warm rooms. Try *Asplenium nidus*, *A. bulbiferum*, *Cyrtomium falcatum*, *Davallia canariensis*, *Nephrolepis exaltata*, *Pellaea rotundifolia*, *Platycerium bifurcatum*, *Pteris cretica*, *P. ensiformis* and *P. tremula*.

Palms make an interesting group, too, being suitable for living-room conditions, provided they have sufficient humidity, and they will not object to shady spots. There are several genera freely available like *Chamaedorea, Chamaerops, Howea, Neanthe and Phoenix*.

Even sansevierias could be grouped together. There is not only the very well-known *Sansevieria trifasciata* 'Laurentii', the mother-in-law's tongue, but also lower-growing kinds like *S. trifasciata* 'Hahnii', which forms rosettes of leaves up to 15 cm (6 in) high. There are gold and silver variegated forms of this – 'Golden Hahnii' and 'Silver Hahnii'. There are several other sansevierias not so freely available, but it may be possible to buy them from a succulent specialist. Try to obtain *S. cylindrica* whose 1 m (3 ft) long leaves are cylindrical and taper to a point. There are several other varieties of *S. trifasciata* which you may come across. As sansevierias are succulent plants they can be grown in a dry atmosphere. They are suitable for normal living-room conditions but must have very bright light and some sun if they are to make good growth.

COLOUR SCHEMES TO MATCH THE ROOM

Another way to group plants is in single colours, the idea of this being that the group matches the colour scheme of the room. For instance, if the colour scheme of a room is red then you could create a group of plants with red foliage and flowers. Purple-leaved plants could be included, too, particularly those with reddish purple foliage. In a blue room you could create a blue group, and so on.

To make plant selection easy I have listed below some houseplants in colour groups; these include flowering and foliage plants. Unless otherwise stated bright light and humidity are required, but only slight humidity in cool rooms.

Red plants
FOR COOL ROOMS

Beloperone guttata (Shrimp plant). Pinkish red bracts, flowers virtually all year round.

Calceolaria x *herbeo-hybrida* (Slipper flower). Blooming in spring-early summer, short-term pot plants.

Coleus blumei (Flame nettle). Some varieties have red leaves. Treated as short-term pot plant.

Cuphea ignea (Cigar plant). Tubular flowers from spring until autumn.

Cyclamen persicum. Many varieties have red flowers, which are produced in autumn and winter.

Euphorbia milii (*E. splendens*) (Crown of thorns). Flowering in winter and spring mainly. Takes dry air as it is a succulent.

Hydrangea macrophylla. Some varieties are in shades of red or pink. Flowering in spring and summer; short-term pot plant.

Kalanchoe blossfeldiana. A succulent plant which flowers from winter to early summer. Suitable for dry atmosphere.

Pelargonium. Many varieties of *P. zonale, P. domesticum* (regal pelargonium) and *P. peltatum* (ivy-leaf pelargonium) have red blooms in summer. They need a dry atmosphere and some sunshine.

Primula. There are red varieties of *P. obconica* and *P. malacoides*, which flower in winter/spring. Short-term pot plants.

Rhododendron simsii (Indian azalea). Autumn- and winter-flowering. Several red varieties.

Rochea coccinea. A succulent plant, taking dry air and flowering in spring and summer. Needs sun.

Senecio x *hybridus* (Cineraria). Short-term pot plant flowering in spring.

FOR WARM ROOMS

Aechmea 'Foster's Favorite'. A bromeliad with reddish bronze foliage.

Anthurium. *A. andreanum* (Painter's palette) and *A. scherzerianum* (Flamingo flower) have scarlet spathes in spring, summer and autumn.

Begonia 'Elatior' hybrids. Tuberous begonias blooming in winter. Several red varieties.

Begonia rex. Foliage begonia, several varieties of which have lots of red or pink in the leaves. Tolerates slight shade.

Bougainvillea glabra (Paper flower). A climber, some varieties of which have red bracts. Flowers in summer and needs sunny spot.

Celosia plumosa. Short-term pot plant, flowering in summer.

Codiaeum variegatum pictum (Croton). Foliage plant, several varieties with plenty of red in the leaves.

Cordyline terminalis. Leaves are bronze-red to purple. The variety 'Rededge' has reddish-purple and green foliage.

Euphorbia pulcherrima (Poinsettia). Large red bracts in winter; a short-term pot plant, popular at Christmas time.

Gynura aurantiaca. Foliage plant, whose leaves are densely covered with purple hairs.

Hibiscus rosa-sinensis. Large red flowers in summer and autumn. Needs some sunshine.

Impatiens wallerana (Busy lizzie). Many with red flowers, blooming throughout summer. Very bright light needed for best flowering.

Iresine herbstii (Bloodleaf). A foliage plant with red stems and leaves.

Philodendron 'Burgundy'. Reddish bronze stems and leaves, the young leaves having the best colour.

Saintpaulia ionantha (African violet). Many varieties have red flowers, mainly in spring, summer and autumn.

Setcreasea purpurea (Purple heart). Rich purple foliage.

Streptocarpus. Some of the hybrid streptocarpus have red or deep pink flowers which are produced over a long period in summer. 'Diana' is deep cerise and 'Paula' is reddish purple.

Blue plants
FOR COOL ROOMS

Campanula isophylla (Bellflower). Produces a long succession of flowers in summer/autumn.

Eucalyptus globulus (Blue gum). Foliage plant with glaucous foliage. Renew plants frequently from seeds.

Exacum affine (Arabian violet). Small flowers in summer/autumn; a short-term pot plant.

Heliotropium (Heliotrope). A short-term summer-flowering plant. Renew annually from cuttings.

Hydrangea macrophylla. Some varieties have blue flowers, flowering period being spring and summer. Short-term pot plants.

Plumbago capensis (Cape leadwort). A climber flowering in summer and autumn.

Senecio × hybridus (Cineraria). A short-term pot plant flowering in spring.

FOR WARM ROOMS

Brunfelsia calycina. Evergreen shrub flowering in summer and autumn.

Saintpaulia ionantha (African violet). Many varieties have blue flowers, these appearing mainly in spring, summer and autumn.

Streptocarpus. Some of the hybrid streptocarpus have blue flowers, which are produced over a long period in the summer. Some recommended varieties are 'Constant Nymph', 'Louise' and 'Margaret'.

Yellow plants
FOR COOL ROOMS

Calceolaria × herbeo-hybrida (Slipper flower). Blooms in spring/early summer; short-term pot plant.

Chrysanthemum. Dwarf pot chrysanthemum, yellow being one of the main colours, a short-term pot plant available all year round.

Sansevieria trifasciata 'Golden Hahnii'. A foliage plant with golden-variegated foliage. Tolerates a dry atmosphere. Suitable for direct sun.

Sansevieria trifasciata 'Laurentii' (Mother-in-law's tongue). Popular plant with yellow-edged leaves.

Senecio macroglossus 'Variegatus'. A climber or trailer with yellow-blotched foliage. Tolerates dry air well.

FOR WARM ROOMS

Aphelandra squarrosa 'Louisae' (Zebra plant). Flower heads consist of yellow bracts, generally appearing in autumn or winter. The leaves have creamy veins.

Calathea crocata. Calatheas are generally grown for their foliage but this one is essentially a flowering plant, producing deep yellow blooms. It has recently become available in garden centres, florists etc., at least in the UK.

Celosia plumosa. A short-term pot plant flowering in summer. Should be raised annually from seeds sown in the spring.

Codiaeum variegatum pictum (Croton). Some varieties of this popular foliage plant have lots of yellow or gold in the leaves.

Dracaena fragrans 'Massangeana'. This is a popular foliage plant, with deep green leaves which have a wide golden stripe down the centre.

Heptapleurum arboricola 'Variegata' (Umbrella tree or parasol plant). A foliage plant whose

Another good choice of pot holder for an African violet. One cannot go wrong with white or pastel coloured pot holders.

finger-like leaves are heavily splashed with bright yellow.

Iresine herbstii 'Aureoreticulata'. A foliage plant with green leaves which are veined or blotched with yellow. Best to raise new plants annually from cuttings.

Pachystachys lutea (Lollipop plant). Flower heads consist of spikes of yellow bracts, through which appear small white tubular flowers. Flowering is in spring and summer. Has only recently become available as a houseplant in the UK.

Peperomia obtusifolia 'Green Gold' (Pepper elder). A foliage plant with light green leaves, which are boldly edged with yellowish cream. Light shade is acceptable.

Scindapsus aureus (Devil's ivy). A climber or trailer grown for its yellow-blotched leaves. The variety 'Golden Queen' is heavily variegated with golden-yellow.

Syngonium podophyllum 'Green Gold' (Goosefoot plant). A climber or trailer with yellow-mottled foliage.

White and green plants

White and green groups create a 'cool' atmosphere and of course any foliage plants with plain green leaves can be included, so I have omitted them from this list. Instead I have concentrated on plants with white flowers and with white and green variegated or striped foliage.

FOR COOL ROOMS

Campanula isophylla 'Alba' (Bellflower). Produces a long succession of white flowers in the summer and autumn.

Chlorophytum comosum 'Variegatum' (Spider plant). One of the most popular foliage houseplants, with grassy leaves striped green and white. Plantlets are produced at the tips of old flower stems. Tolerates some shade as well as partial sun.

Hedera (Ivy). There are several variegated varieties of the common English ivy, *Hedera helix*, like 'Glacier'. Then there is the larger-leaved variegated Canary Island ivy, *H. canariensis* 'Gloire de Marengo' (or 'Variegata'), a very popular houseplant. Ivies are used as climbers and trailers.

Hoya (Wax flower). *H. bella* is a bushy plant producing starry white flowers with red centres in summer. Needs some sunshine. *H. carnosa* is a climbing species with waxy white blooms in summer. Also needs some sunshine for optimum growth.

Jasminum polyanthum (Jasmine). Heavily scented white flowers in winter and spring. A climbing plant that likes some sunshine.

Sparmannia africana. A large shrub producing white, golden-centred flowers in summer.

Tradescantia fluminensis 'Quicksilver' (Wandering Jew). In my opinion the best of the tradescantias, whose leaves are boldly striped with green and silvery white. It is a trailing plant.

FOR WARM ROOMS

Aglaonema commutatum (Chinese evergreen). Several varieties have silvery or white variegated foliage, like 'White Rajah' ('Pseudobracteatum'), and 'Silver Queen'.

Dieffenbachia maculata (Dumb cane). Popular foliage plant with deep green leaves blotched with white. The cultivar 'Exotica' is very heavily blotched.

Dracaena deremensis. This foliage plant and its varieties such as 'Bausei' and 'Warneckii', have sword-shaped green and white striped leaves and are very popular houseplants.

Ficus radicans 'Variegata' (Creeping fig). A trailing foliage plant with white-edged leaves.

Pandanus veitchii (Screw pine). The sword-shaped leaves of this distinctive foliage plant are deep green with white stripes. They are edged with hooked 'teeth'.

Peperomia caperata 'Variegata' (Pepper elder). Dwarf foliage plant with heart-shaped crinkled leaves, light green with a broad white margin.

Pilea cadierei (Aluminium plant). A popular foliage plant whose leaves are heavily splashed with silver. 'Nana' is a shorter, more compact variety.

Scindapsus aureus 'Marble Queen' (Devil's ivy). A climbing or trailing foliage plant whose leaves are heavily variegated with white.

Spathiphyllum wallisii (White sails). Produces pure white spathes in summer. The variety 'Mauna Loa' is taller and has larger spathes.

Stephanotis floribunda. In summer this climber produces heavily scented, waxy white flowers. It is not one of the easiest houseplants to grow but most people like to have a go. Really good light is needed together with steady warmth and high humidity.

Zantedeschia aethiopica (Arum lily). Produces white spathes in spring or early summer. Worth searching for is the variety 'Green Goddess' with green and white spathes. Zantedeschia is also suitable for growing in cool rooms.

11
HANGING HOUSEPLANTS

To make maximum use of space, and to add interest and colour on higher levels (see also Chapter 13), plants can be grown in hanging containers of various kinds. Some plants, in fact, need to be elevated due to their habit – they may be pendulous or trailing, or they may have colourful undersides to the leaves, which would not be seen if the plants were to be grown at lower levels, as on tables and window-sills.

CONTAINERS

Types

The containers which immediately spring to mind are hanging baskets, but I have reservations about these. The traditional wire hanging baskets, which are lined with sphagnum moss, are not suitable for indoor use due to risk of drips when watering. There are available, however, rigid, moulded-plastic hanging baskets which have built-in drip trays. These are mainly intended for outdoor use, being ideal for balconies etc., but they can be used in rooms, although I would not say they are particularly attractive, even though they are functional.

I much prefer some kind of hanging pot-holder. Looking around various shops I notice that macramé pot-holders are becoming more readily available. I have now invested in several of these, one of which holds two ceramic pots, one above the other, and I have hung it from a beam in my lounge. Other smaller ones which take only one pot I have hung in window recesses. If you are contemplating another hobby why not consider macramé? It is an up-and-coming pastime and you could make your own hanging pot-holders.

In garden centres etc., you will also find other kinds of hanging pot-holders, the pot-holders themselves being in various materials such as plastic, ceramic, wood, etc. I like the idea of pot-holders, rather than baskets, as plants can be easily re-arranged or replaced. This is more difficult with baskets for the plants are planted directly in them.

Hanging pot-holders and baskets can be supported with ornamental brackets – I favour black wrought iron, especially for cottages, or cottage-style houses, but there are plenty of modern brackets available for contemporary homes.

It is not necessary even to use baskets or pot-holders for some plants – epiphytic plants (those which grow on trees in the wild) can be mounted on pieces of cork bark, natural bark or even on slabs of wood, these being hung in suitable places. Plants such as *Platycerium bifurcatum*, the stag's horn fern (Fig. 8), and epiphytic bromeliads, including the air plants or small atmospheric tillandsias, can be grown in this way. The tillandsias should simply be tied on to the bark or wood as they have few if any roots and must not be grown in compost. Other plants can be removed from their pots and have some of the compost teased away, but some is left around the roots which are then held in place with live sphagnum moss. This ball of compost and moss is then tied to the bark or wood. Even better than tying is to stretch a piece of small-mesh black plastic netting over the root area, this being held in place behind the bark or wood with drawing pins. Netting effectively holds in the moss and compost.

The air plants or tillandsias are watered by spraying them daily in warm conditions, or weekly in cool conditions, with plain water.

Fig. 8. Epiphytic plants, like *Platycerium bifurcatum* (the stag's horn fern), can be grown on pieces of cork bark or natural bark hung in suitable parts of a room.

alcoves. They can also be hung from beams and from ornamental brackets fixed to walls.

There can be a few problems with this method of display. High up in a centrally heated room the atmosphere can be very hot and dry, so plants are liable to dry out rapidly, necessitating daily checks for water requirements. Plants which need moist air must be mist sprayed daily or twice daily to prevent the edges of the leaves drying up and turning brown.

PLANTS FOR WARM ROOMS

These need to be grown in a warm living room, with a minimum temperature at night of 15.5°C (60°F), although some will tolerate a minimum of 13°C (55°F), like asparagus, callisia, nephrolepis, plectranthus and setcreasea. They also need high humidity.

Asparagus densiflorus 'Myers' (FOXTAIL ASPARAGUS)
Seemingly not a likely candidate for hanging containers, for when young the bright green foxtail-like plumes are erect, but older stems arch over, and the plant then certainly looks good above head height. Place in light shade. Allow compost to partially dry out between watering, and be sparing with water in winter. Do not allow compost to dry right out, though, or the 'leaves' may drop. Grow in soil-based potting compost and feed well in the growing period.

Callisia elegans
A relative of the tradescantias, or wandering Jews, which can also be used in hanging containers. However, I consider callisia a more attractive looking plant, with its olive-green foliage boldly striped with white. The undersides of the leaves are purple, not seen unless the plant is elevated. The plant needs really bright light; allow the compost to partially dry out before applying water. In winter the stems should be cut back. Grow in soil-based compost.

Other plants are watered by placing the bark or wood in a bowl of water until the compost and moss are thoroughly moist. Allow to drain completely (say overnight) before re-hanging. Slabs of wood and bark can be hung up with string, wire or decorative rope.

Where to hang containers
Light-loving plants are best hung in recessed or alcove windows so that they receive maximum light. Shade-loving plants are suitable for positions further into the room, such as

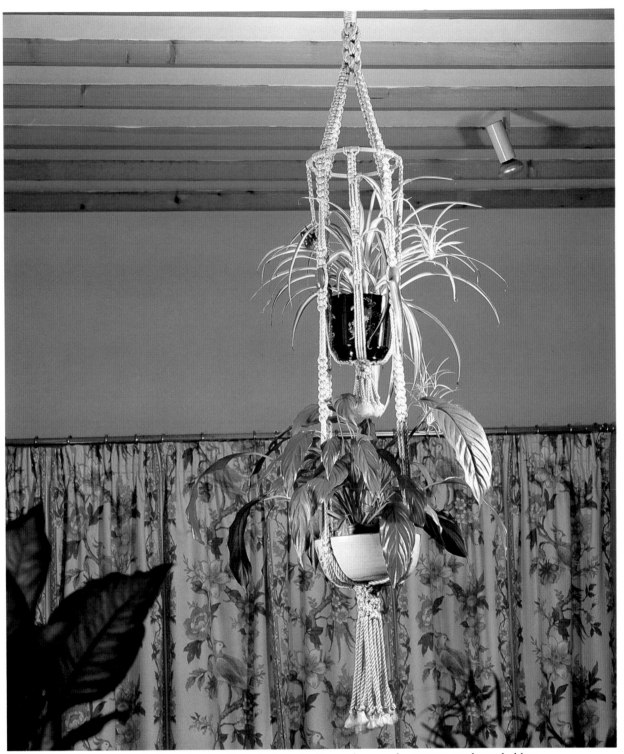

I am a great believer in elevating plants and often make use of macrame-work pot holders. This one supports a variegated chlorophytum and a spathiphyllum.

Davallia canariensis (DEER'S FOOT FERN)
This popular fern has lacy mid-green fronds about 30 cm (12 in) long, and they are finely divided, giving a lacy appearance. Grow in shallow containers of soilless compost, in bright light, including sun if not too strong. Keep steadily moist all year round, and give monthly feeds in summer. This is an epiphytic plant, so is a natural choice for elevation.

Mikania ternata (PLUSH VINE)
This is a newcomer, at least in Britain, and well worth trying if you come across it in the shops. It's a trailer, with palmate hairy leaves, green, flushed purple, on top and purple below. It is a vigorous plant and easily grown in the right conditions. Keep the compost steadily moist and place in light shade.

Nephrolepis exaltata (SWORD FERN)
See also Chapter 13. Grow in soilless compost, water moderately all year round and place in light shade.

Oplismenus hirtellus 'Variegatus'
A trailing plant with narrow grassy leaves attractively striped green, white and pink. It is best renewed frequently from cuttings which are easily rooted in spring or early summer. Keep well watered in growing season, but ease up in winter; grow in soil-based compost and position in bright light.

Peperomia scandens 'Variegata' (PEPPER ELDER)
A trailing peperomia with waxy, green and yellow variegated foliage. The stems can attain a length of 60 cm (24 in). As overwatering can cause root rot, apply water only when the compost has almost dried out. Grow in light shade, or in bright light but not direct sun. Best in soilless potting compost.

Plectranthus oertendahlii (CANDLE PLANT)
Vigorous trailing plant with deep green foliage, enhanced with prominent white veins, purple below. Water well, except in winter when the compost should be allowed to partially dry out. Grow in soil-based compost and place in light shade.

Scindapsus aureus (DEVIL'S IVY)
See also Chapter 13. A very popular trailing (or climbing) plant. There are several varieties, with leaves variegated yellow or white, like 'Golden Queen' and 'Marble Queen'. These are a bit more tricky to grow than the species. Grow in soil-based compost and keep out of direct sun.

Setcreasea purpurea (PURPLE HEART)
A trailer with 10–15 cm (4–6 in) long, lanceolate bright purple leaves. Grow in bright light but avoid direct strong sun. Allow compost to partially dry out between waterings. Grow in soil-based compost. Renew plants frequently from cuttings which root easily in spring or summer.

Stenotaphrum secundatum 'Variegatum' (BUFFALO GRASS)
A grassy plant with cream foliage, striped with green, giving overall a very light effect. The stems will root into the compost if they come in contact with it – a good method of propagation. Provide bright light, plenty of water in the growing season, far less in winter, and grow in soil-based compost. Only needs a shallow container.

Syngonium podophyllum (GOOSE FOOT)
See also Chapter 13. A trailer or climber. There are several variegated varieties worth searching for like 'Green Gold', 'Emerald Gem' and 'Imperial White'. Water sparingly in winter, moderately at other times; place in light shade, and grow in peaty compost.

PLANTS FOR COOL ROOMS
These are best grown in cool rooms, with a temperature range of 7–13°C (45–55°F). Correspondingly the atmosphere must be dry.

Campanula isophylla (BELLFLOWER)
See also Chapter 13. Grow in bright light,

water very sparingly in winter and trim back old flowered stems.

Hedera helix (COMMON IVY)

See also Chapter 13. There are many varieties of the common ivy, and they are hardy plants, suitable even for an unheated room. Some have green foliage, like 'Chicago', 'Cristata', 'Sagittaefolia' and 'Ivalace', while others are variegated, such as 'Glacier', 'Marmorata', 'Jubilee' and 'Lutzii'. Never allow the compost to remain wet or the roots may rot. Be very sparing with water in winter.

Pelargonium peltatum (IVY-LEAF PELARGONIUM)

Used more for outdoor display in summer than as a room plant, nevertheless the ivy-leaf pelargonium varieties can be recommended if they are grown in really bright light, including some sun. The habit is trailing and the leaves are indeed ivy-shaped. Flowering is prolific in summer, blooms being in shades of pink, red, mauve and also white. Water normally in growing period but very sparingly in winter. Grow in soil-based compost. Renew regularly from cuttings rooted in summer.

Senecio macroglossus 'Variegatus' (WAX VINE)

A trailer or climber with ivy-shaped waxy fleshy leaves, green but heavily variegated cream. Grow it in really bright light, including sun, but not too strong. Water very sparingly in winter, and only moderately during the growing period. Grow in a very well-drained soil-based compost – best to add extra grit or coarse sand.

12

CLIMBING PLANTS

There is a surprisingly wide range of climbing plants suitable for growing indoors, enabling one to make maximum use of vertical space. All too often the upper parts of rooms are devoid of plant life.

HOW TO USE CLIMBERS EFFECTIVELY

One way in which I like to use climbers is to frame windows with them. They are easily supported with wires or cords, which can be secured with steel screw eyes.

Large climbers can also be trained up walls in a similar way, using screw eyes and strong cords or wires. The stems of the plants should be tied in to these supports as they grow with soft garden string, preferably coloured green.

Climbers can also be trained up room dividers, particularly the open trellis-work type, provided there is sufficient light within the room.

Climbing plants can even be used to form living screens or room dividers. For this purpose each plant could be grown in a square planter or container and trained up canes or a moss pole (see below). The plants are placed in a row to form the screen.

SUPPORTS FOR FREE-STANDING CLIMBERS

Unless the plants are to be trained to walls, room dividers etc., they will need some independent form of support. Many people will use bamboo canes, inserting two or three around the edge of the pot and loosely tying the stems to them with soft string.

Another method is to use a framework of bamboo canes, which can be made to any shape desired. It is also possible to buy wire framework for climbers, popularly known as 'pot trellis'. Generally this is made from plastic-coated wire or steel. Generally these proprietary supports are not very large and only suitable for small climbers.

Wire hoops make excellent supports for some climbers like bougainvillea, hedera, hoya, jasminum, passiflora, plumbago, stephanotis and thunbergia. I find that the flowering plants often bloom much more freely if their stems are trained horizontally rather than vertically. This method also ensures that tall climbers can be better contained if space is limited. You will need some really thick galvanized wire to make the hoops. This is simply bent to the required shape, ensuring two 'stems' at the bottom which are pushed into the pot. The hoop may need the additional support of a few vertical bamboo canes.

A cylinder of wire netting, again supported with a few bamboo canes, makes a suitable support for some climbers, such as cissus, hedera (ivy) and thunbergia.

Moss poles are recommended for supporting some of the heavier climbers, including those which form roots on their stems – aerial roots. Plants which can be supported in this way include × fatshedera, hedera, monstera (Fig. 9), philodendron, scindapsus and syngonium. The plants which produce aerial roots – like the philodendron and monstera – will root into the moss and support themselves.

Moss poles of various heights can be bought from garden centres and florists, but you may wish to make your own, which is quite easy. You can also make them thicker

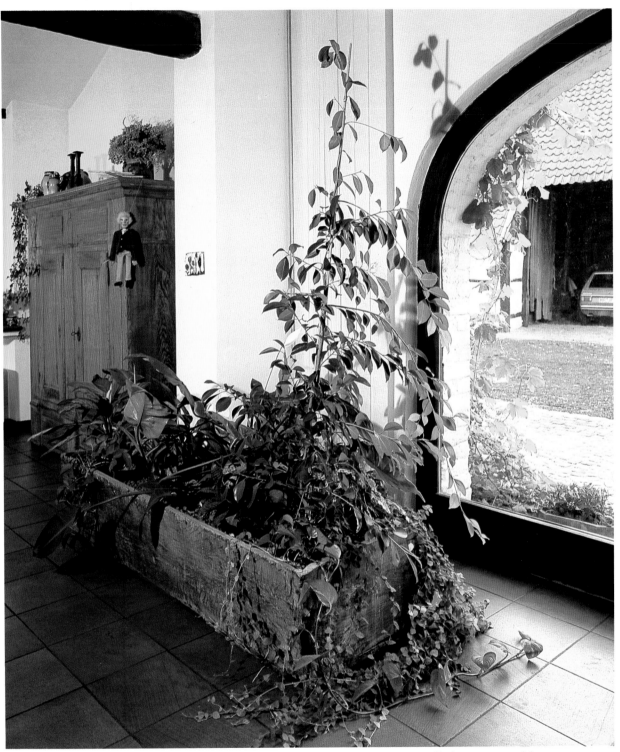
An attractive way of arranging a group of plants in a 'planter', with a tall plant at one end (a *Ficus benjamina*), grading down to shorter plants towards the other end.

than proprietary ones, which I find is an advantage, particularly for tall heavy plants.

To make a moss pole, use a broom handle of suitable length and insert this well into the pot. Place over this a cylinder of small-mesh wire netting, extending it below the compost surface. Then pack the cylinder with live sphagnum moss, which you should be able to obtain from a florist. A small pot should be inserted in the top of the wire cylinder and rested on top of the broom handle. This provides an easy means of keeping the moss moist (it should be kept moist at all times) as you simply pour water into the pot and it will trickle down through the moss. If you do not

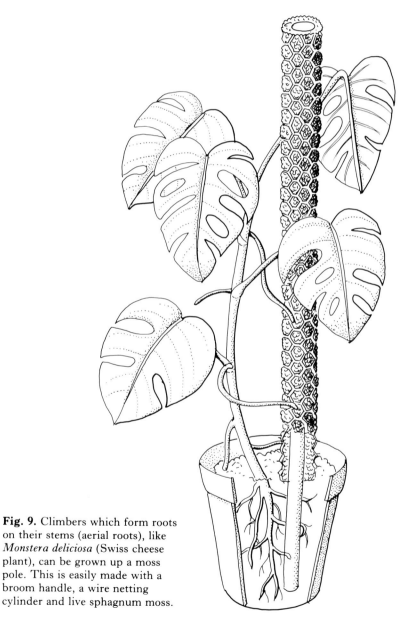

Fig. 9. Climbers which form roots on their stems (aerial roots), like *Monstera deliciosa* (Swiss cheese plant), can be grown up a moss pole. This is easily made with a broom handle, a wire netting cylinder and live sphagnum moss.

want to use this method, keep the moss moist by spraying it as necessary with a hand sprayer. Aerial roots, which support the plants, should be guided into the moss as they grow. If plants do not produce aerial roots tie them loosely to the pole with soft green garden string.

SOME POPULAR CLIMBING PLANTS

A number of climbing plants have already been discussed in other chapters. These are as follows (chapter numbers in brackets): bougainvillea (10), hedera (10, 11), hoya (10), jasminum (10), philodendron (9, 10), plumbago (10), scindapsus (10, 11), stephanotis (10) and syngonium (10, 11).

Others I can recommend are as follows:

Cissus Vigorous evergreen foliage plants. *C. antarctica* is the popular kangaroo vine with deep green shiny leaves. *C. discolor*, the begonia vine, has velvety leaves banded with green and silver. *C. rhombifolia (Rhoicissus rhomboidea)*, the grape ivy, has bright green foliage. Grow them in shade or good light. They are suitable for cool or warm rooms (warm for *C. discolor*) and need humidity.

Clerodendrum thomsoniae (Glory bower) White and red flowers in summer. Needs a warm room, very bright light and high humidity. Rest in winter in a cool room.

× **Fatshedera lizei** Fast-growing foliage plant with lobed green leaves. Suitable for cool or warm rooms and shade; needs moderate humidity.

Monstera deliciosa (Swiss cheese plant) Large deeply cut and perforated leaves. A rapid tall grower. Needs a warm room, high humidity and subdued light.

Passiflora caerulea (Blue passion flower) Blue flowers in summer/autumn. Cool room (keep cool in winter, especially), bright light including some sun, humidity in warm conditions.

Philodendron I have already recommended several. Others you may like to try are *P. bipennifolium, P. erubescens, P. hastatum, P. imbe, P. laciniatum (P. pedatum), P. scandens* and *P. 'Tuxla'*.

Thunbergia alata (Black-eyed Susan) An annual climber raised from seeds sown in the spring. Orange or yellow flowers produced in profusion during the summer, each with a dark centre. Needs a temperature of not less than 10°C (50°F), very bright light, including some sun, and humidity in warm conditions.

13

DISPLAYING PLANTS ON WALLS

In many homes walls are adorned with pictures, photographs, ornamental plates and the like, but rarely with plants. We Britons seem to keep plants at a low level, ending our displays at window-sill height. This is a pity, for plants positioned fairly high up on a wall can create a dramatic room feature.

Americans will undoubtedly be more familiar with this method of displaying plants: indeed, I think it is safe to say that the idea originated in the USA.

All kinds of plants can be displayed on walls, not only the obvious trailing and pendulous kinds, but also upright subjects and epiphytic plants. What more natural position for epiphytes, which are tree-dwelling plants in the wild.

Not only are large expanses of wall suitable for this method of display, but alcoves, too – a wall display can be as large or as small as you wish.

SUPPORTS FOR THE PLANTS

Basically the system comprises trellis panels fixed to the wall which support plastic potholders. Plants (in their pots) are then simply placed in the holders.

There are various kinds of trellis panels which can be used and obviously they must be suitable for use indoors. There is quite a range of shapes and sizes available, too.

I use plastic-coated steel panels, in white, which look rather smart and they come complete with nylon brackets for securing them to the wall. The brackets hold the panels about 2.5 cm (1 in) away from the wall, which is necessary to ensure air circulation. If you hunt around garden centres you should find special plastic-coated steel brackets for the

pot-holders, which simply hook over the horizontal bars of the trellis.

If you cannot find these brackets, then it is quite easy to make your own from heavy duty plastic-coated or galvanized wire. Basically they consist of a circle (which holds the potholder) and a couple of hooks. The whole thing can be formed from a single length of wire.

Other kinds of trellis can be used if desired. There is no reason why wooden trellis should not be used and, of course, it can be painted to match the decor of the room. I have seen bamboo trellis panels on sale and these would certainly look good in the right setting. If you are a DIY enthusiast it would be a comparatively simple matter to make wooden trellis panels, ideally using the square grid pattern. Bear in mind that you do not need very heavy trellis – wooden laths would be ideal for making up panels.

ARRANGING AND CARING FOR PLANTS

I like to have a very mixed collection of plants on trellis and include trailing kinds as well as more upright specimens. They are arranged to give a pleasing and natural-looking effect. For instance, I might have one or two trailers fairly high up on the trellis so that they tumble down between more upright plants lower down. Plants with an arching habit of growth, such as *Platycerium bifurcatum*, the stag's horn fern, and some of the bromeliads with arching foliage, look most natural when placed fairly high up so that they are viewed as they would be in the wild.

I find it is best not to be sparing with plants – place them fairly close together to create a

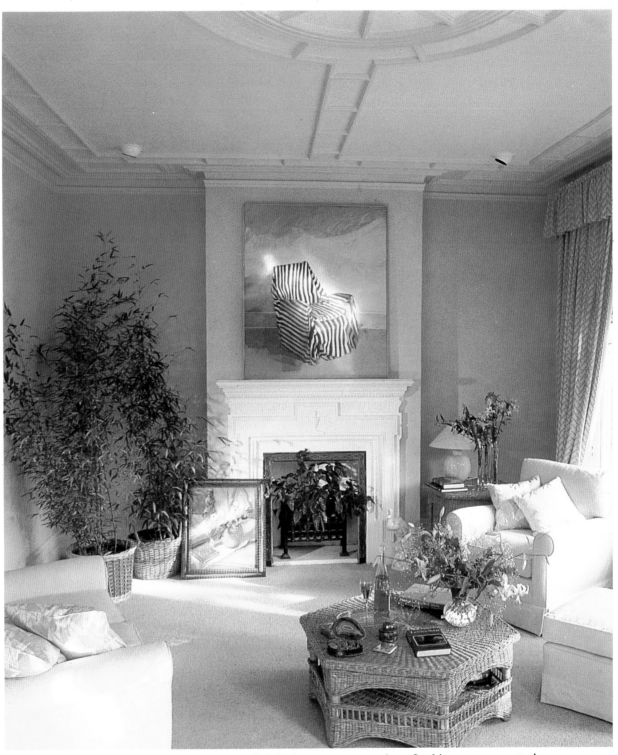

Restrained use of plants may be called for in some room settings. In this corner are potted
bamboos, which would be considered temporary residents.

73

dense 'jungle atmosphere'. The majority of plants I use are foliage kinds, but I also include one or two flowering subjects in season to add splashes of colour.

Remember that the plants are easily moved, so the display can be changed and altered around quite quickly. As with any group of plants do ensure that all plants need the same conditions in respect of temperature, light and humidity.

There can be problems with this method of display. In a warm room, such as the living room or dining area, you will find that conditions become very warm higher up in the room. Of course, this is due to the fact that heat rises. The problem is most acute in centrally heated rooms, when the atmosphere is also very dry. In these conditions plants need very much more care and attention than those on lower levels. The compost dries out rapidly so plants should be checked daily for water requirements. Also one must ensure sufficient humidity, and this means mist spraying the plants daily in warm conditions – or maybe even twice daily. Of course, one way around this is to choose plants which revel in a dry atmosphere, such as the desert cacti and succulents. There are, in fact, several desert cacti with a trailing habit of growth, together with a good selection of other succulent plants.

RECOMMENDED PLANTS

As I have indicated, virtually any kind of indoor plant can be displayed on wall trellis – it is not necessary to use only trailing kinds. However, you might like to consider the following, which I have successfully grown on trellis.

Flowering plants

Anthurium andreanum. Scarlet or orange-red spathes. Minimum temperature of 15.5°C (60°F) and high humidity.

Campanula isophylla (Bellflower). Blue or white flowers. Suitable for cool room and slight humidity.

Hypocyrta glabra (Clog plant). Orange flowers.

Minimum temperature 10°C (50°F); high humidity.

Impatiens wallerana hybrids (Busy lizzie). Many varieties and colours, with long flowering season. Minimum temperature 10°C (50°F); high humidity.

Spathiphyllum wallisii (White sails). Large white spathes. Minimum temperature 13°C (55°F); high humidity.

Foliage plants

Asparagus densiflorus 'Sprengeri' (Asparagus fern). Trailing habit. Minimum temperature 10°C (50°F); humid atmosphere.

Begonia serratipetala. Reddish lobed and toothed leaves. Minimum temperature 15.5°C (60°F); high humidity.

Bromeliads. I have tried many of these, mainly epiphytic, like the smaller billbergias (the easy *B. nutans* has arching foliage); guzmannias; nidulariums; tillandsias (including the atmospheric tillandsias or 'air plants', mounted on pieces of driftwood or bark, and hung on the trellis); and vriesias (especially *V. splendens* with brown-banded foliage). Minimum temperature of 10°C (50°F); high humidity.

Chlorophytum comosum 'Variegatum' (Spider plant). This ever-popular plant with variegated foliage needs a minimum temperature of 7°C (45°F); humidity appreciated.

Ficus. Any of the trailing kinds like *F. pumila* and *F. radicans* 'Variegata'. Minimum temperature 15.5°C (60°F); high humidity.

Hedera helix (Common ivy). Green or variegated foliage. Suitable for cool rooms, humidity in warm conditions.

Maranta leuconeura 'Kerchoveana'. (Prayer plant). Brown-spotted foliage. Minimum temperature 10°C (50°F); high humidity.

Nephrolepis exaltata (Sword fern). Bright green arching fronds. Minimum temperature 13°C (55°F); high humidity.

Peperomia (Pepper elder). Any variety is suitable. Minimum temperature 15.5°C (60°F); high humidity.

Philodendron scandens. Heart-shaped leaves. Minimum temperature 15.5°C (60°F); high humidity.

Platycerium bifurcatum (Stag's horn fern). Antler-like fronds. Minimum temperature 15.5°C (60°F); high humidity.

Scindapsus aureus (Devil's ivy). Yellow-blotched leaves. Minimum temperature 15.5°C 60°F); high humidity.

Syngonium podophyllum (Goose foot). Variegated arrow-shaped foliage. Minimum temperature 15.5°C (60°F); high humidity.

Tolmiea menziesii (Pick-a-back plant). Produces plantlets on leaves. Hardy, ideal for cool room. Low humidity in cool conditions.

Cacti and succulents

Forest cacti. Try the epiphyllum hybrids or orchid cacti; *Rhipsalidopsis gaertneri* and *R. rosea*; rhipsalis; and *Schlumbergera* × *buckleyi*, the Christmas cactus. All of these are epiphytic, need a temperature of 10°C (50°F) in winter, warmth in summer and high humidity.

Desert cacti and other succulents. Try those with a pendulous habit, such as *Ceropegia woodii, Senecio rowleyanus, Sedum morganianum* and selenicereus. These need a dry atmosphere and should be kept cool in winter – 10°C (50°F) or slightly below – and warm in summer.

14

PLANT TREES

Very rarely in the UK do we see indoor plants grown in any other way than in pots, but with the recent introduction of a group of bromeliads known as air plants (atmospheric tillandsias) we are literally forced to look to other methods, for air plants absolutely refuse to grow in compost. They have few, if any, roots and absorb moisture, via scales on their leaves, from the atmosphere.

A superb way of displaying the atmospheric tillandsias is on a well-branched tree branch, for the sake of convenience referred to as a 'plant tree'. A plant tree can make a stunning room feature and will be the main talking point of all visitors.

It is not only the air plants, though, that are suitable for growing on plant trees, but other epiphytic plants also. Epiphytes are plants which grow on trees in the wild. Some ferns are epiphytic, like *Platycerium bifurcatum*, the stag's horn fern. So, too, are the forest cacti, like species of rhipsalis, epiphyllum, rhipsalidopsis and schlumbergera. Many orchids are epiphytic, together with a wide range of bromeliads apart from the air plants. All of these make excellent subjects for a plant tree.

MAKING A PLANT TREE

The tree can be any height desired, from a few feet to ceiling height. The branch chosen should in itself be well branched and it must be perfectly sound, in other words, not starting to rot, or its life will be reduced.

How do we support the tree branch? Choose a suitably large, ornamental container, either square or round, position the branch in the middle, holding it upright with temporary supports, and then fill the container almost to the top with mortar. When this has set remove the supports and, for aesthetic reasons, spread a layer of peat or shredded bark over the surface of the mortar.

POSITIONING THE PLANTS

The small atmospheric tillandsias or air plants are very easy to place on the tree: they can be gently wedged in crotches, or they can be loosely tied in place, using nylon thread (Fig. 10). Do not tie tightly or the thread will cut into the plants and damage them. It is also possible to buy, from a specialist bromeliad nursery in the UK a special glue to actually stick the plants to the tree. Do not use glue, though, if you cannot obtain the correct one, for some types can damage plants.

Other epiphytic plants have roots and are generally bought as pot-grown specimens. These should be removed from their pots and most of the compost teased away from the roots. The roots can then be set in 'cushions' of live sphagnum moss on the tree, with the moss held in place with a few twists of thin copper wire, plastic-coated wire or nylon thread. If the top part of the plant needs securing, then judiciously tie it in to a branch with nylon thread.

It may be possible to gently wedge some plants into crotches formed by the branches. It is much easier to start off with small young plants, rather than trying to mount large heavy specimens. The young plants will eventually support themselves as they send out roots, which attach themselves to the tree.

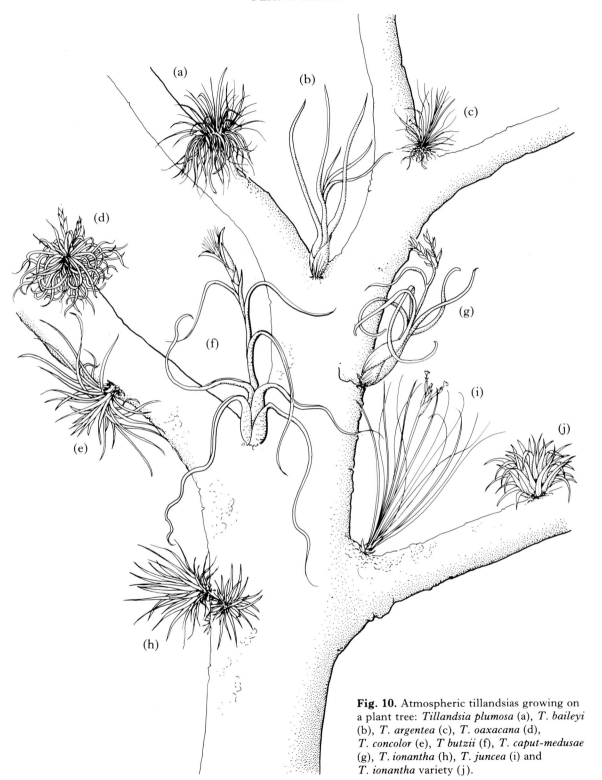

Fig. 10. Atmospheric tillandsias growing on
a plant tree: *Tillandsia plumosa* (a), *T. baileyi*
(b), *T. argentea* (c), *T. oaxacana* (d),
T. concolor (e), *T butzii* (f), *T. caput-medusae*
(g), *T. ionantha* (h), *T. juncea* (i) and
T. ionantha variety (j).

CARE OF THE PLANTS

The majority of plants that are used on a plant tree will be happy in a warm room. The bromeliads, though, will take quite low temperatures in the winter – as low as 7°C (45°F). Good light is needed, but none of the plants should be subjected to direct strong sunshine. Bromeliads and cacti like very airy conditions. High humidity is needed in warm conditions, far less in a cool atmosphere. Humidity is provided by spraying the plants and the tree.

Spraying is also the method of watering. The tree, moss and the plants themselves are sprayed with a hand sprayer. The moss (and therefore the root systems) should be kept steadily moist. As already mentioned, the atmospheric tillandsias absorb moisture through their leaves, so must be sprayed regularly with water. In warm conditions spray daily, while in cool conditions weekly spraying will be sufficient. Do not drench the air plants, simply give them a light spraying. Lime-free water must be used for the air plants and ideally, too, for other epiphytes. Rain-water is, of course, ideal.

Like other plants, epiphytes grown on a plant tree need feeding. During the summer, when they are in full growth, they can be given a foliar feed about once a month, using a liquid fertilizer. Use this only at about one-quarter of the strength recommended by the manufacturer.

Of course, a plant tree is not without its problems – it can drip water after being sprayed. It might, therefore, be sensible to stand it on a flat tray of some kind to catch the drips unless it can be placed, for example, on a quarry-tile floor.

ATMOSPHERIC TILLANDSIAS FOR A PLANT TREE

A limited selection of atmospheric tillandsias can now be bought from garden centres and even from some high-street chain stores in the UK. For a much wider choice, though, you will have to buy from specialist bromeliad nurserymen, of which there are at least two in the UK. They can be bought mail order, plant lists and catalogues being supplied. If you can visit such a nursery, so much the better – it is a truly fascinating experience, quite unlike any other plant nursery.

The following list contains both popular, freely available plants, and some of the more unusual species obtainable only from specialist growers. All are highly recommended and will give much pleasure. They produce flowers, albeit small ones, which are often highly coloured. I have not described the flowers in the list, though, for I feel the main attraction of these plants is the foliage, and indeed the general habits of the plants.

T. argentea This species has fine, thread-like, but stiffish, silvery foliage and is one of the easily available air plants. Should be in every collection.

T. baileyi This plant has a bulbous base and green, curiously contorted leaves. Again it is quite well known and may be found in garden centres.

T. brachycaulos This is a highly colourful species, for its rosette of thin green leaves turns brilliant red if the plant is given bright light. One of the lesser-known species and not likely to be found in garden centres.

T. brachyphylla This produces rosettes of stiff, very silvery leaves and is extremely attractive. For some reason it does not seem to be too well known, either in the UK or in the USA. Nevertheless it is well worth a place in your collection.

T. butzii This is quite a well-known species, with a bulbous base and green contorted leaves. It's easily grown and not difficult to obtain.

T. caput-medusae This is another well-known species with a bulbous base and green contorted leaves. You should be able to pick up this one from a garden centre.

T. geminiflora This species forms a compact rosette of green leaves covered with grey scales. It is easily grown but would have to be bought from a specialist.

T. ionantha Undoubtedly this is one of the best-known and easiest species, being available from garden centres. It forms contorted rosettes of leaves which may be green or silvery.

T. juncea Quite freely available, this species

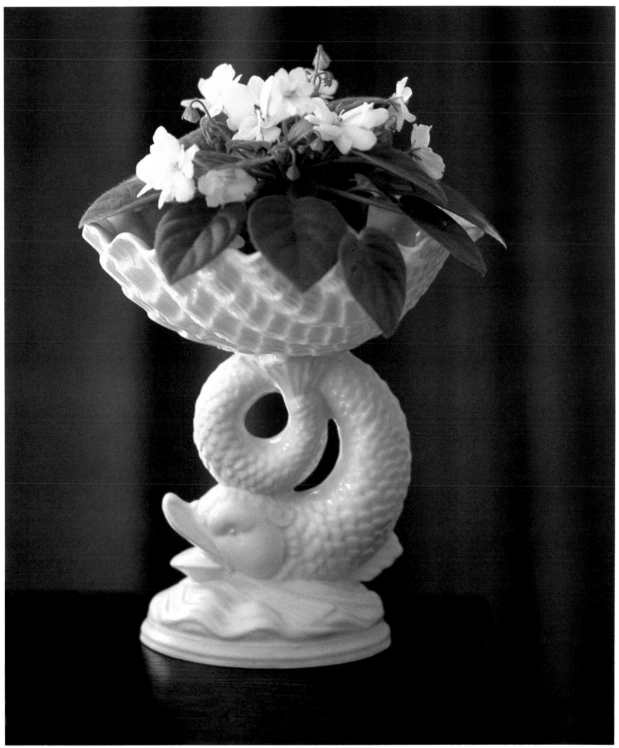

This dolphin vase makes a superb pot holder for a white African violet or saintpaulia, and the plain velvet curtains provide a perfect background.

has long, thin, upright, green, rush-like leaves, and is very easily grown.

T. magnusiana This is a most striking air plant, the thin leaves being held upright and carried in a rosette. They are green, but heavily sprinkled with silver scales, so giving the plant an overall silvery appearance. Available from specialists only.

T. sprengeliana Another species that will have to be searched for, it is a small plant forming a very tight rosette of overlapping short leaves, which are rather contorted. The leaves are green but heavily sprinkled with silvery scales.

T. stricta Available only from specialist growers. It forms dense rosettes of stiff arching grey-green leaves, although the colour of the leaves is variable. It is easy to grow and particularly attractive in flower, with its deep pink bracts.

T. tectorum Forms rosettes of very thin, bright silver leaves. It is best given a bright sunny spot, as it grows in hot sunny places in the wild. Would have to be bought from a specialist.

T. usneoides This species is popularly known as Spanish moss, and consists of masses of thread-like pendulous stems. These are generally greyish green, and 'planting' simply consists of hanging a bunch over a branch. It is starting to appear in garden centres, but you will certainly be able to buy it from a specialist bromeliad grower. Should be in every collection.

15
PLANTS IN WINDOWS

Maximum use should be made of windows for displaying plants – not just the window-sills, but also the space above them. Shelves can be installed above the window-sills on which to stage suitable plants. Some plants, particularly those with thin colourful leaves, are very much enhanced when light shines through them – the colours and patterns showing up particularly well. Such an arrangement of plants is also useful if you want to hide an ugly view.

To prevent cutting out too much light I would suggest that plate-glass shelves are erected (Fig. 11). A local glass supplier should be able to make these for you. The shelves are supported by means of suitable brackets fixed to the window frame.

CHOOSING SUITABLE PLANTS

Of course, plants have to be chosen with care according to the amount of sun the windows receive. There are plenty for sunny windows, in other words, those which face south, west or east. If the sun is too strong for some of them it can be diffused by means of net curtains. It would be advisable to hang these on a rail so that they can be drawn back, for example, when the weather is dull, to provide the plants with maximum light. Some windows – those facing north – will receive no sun so are ideal for plants which like good bright light but not direct sun.

Plants for windows which receive no sun
For this situation there are several plants which would be much enhanced with the light shining through them, including the maidenhair ferns or adiantums with delicate-looking fronds on wiry black stalks. They need a minimum temperature of 15.5°C (60°F) and high humidity. Popular species include *Adiantum raddianum* (*A. cuneatum*), with pale green leaflets, and its varieties 'Gracillimum' and 'Fritz Luthii'; and *A. tenerum* which is similar but taller.

Also suitable are some of the thin-leaved begonias with patterned foliage, like *B.* 'Tiger' and *B.* 'Cleopatra'. Both of these have leaves marbled with bronze. They need the same conditions as adiantums. Also requiring a warm room and high humidity are the varieties of *Maranta leuconeura*, or prayer plant, like 'Erythroneura', 'Kerchoveana' and 'Massangeana'. All have beautifully marked leaves.

Needing a minimum temperature of 18°C (65°F) and very high humidity are the varieties of *Caladium bicolor* which have paper-thin leaves. They are so thin that they are almost transparent and are very brightly coloured – generally multicoloured. Caladiums grow from tuberous roots and the plants are dried off and rested over the winter.

Plants for sunny windows
Many flowering pot plants are best grown in sunny windows but most will need to be protected by means of net curtains from direct very strong sunshine. The same applies to the foliage plants listed here. However, there are some plants which will take direct sun, including cacti and succulents; *Ananas comosus* 'Variegatus', the variegated pineapple; pelargoniums; and sansevierias, of which the dwarf *S. trifasciata* 'Hahnii' and varieties are most suitable for window shelves.

Fig. 11. Some plants, especially those with thin leaves, are much enhanced when light shines through them. They can be displayed on plate-glass shelves installed above the window-sill.

For foliage, some of the abutilons can be recommended, as they have thin variegated leaves through which the light will shine. Try

A. × *hybridum* 'Savitzii' with white and green variegated leaves, and *A. striatum* 'Thompsonii' whose leaves are heavily mottled with yellow. They are suited to cool or warm rooms.

The achimenes are grown for their summer flowers and are among the few members of the *Gesneriaceae* family which can be grown successfully in normal living-room conditions. They need plenty of warmth and humidity, though, and the rhizomes, from which they grow, are dried off for the winter. The tubular or trumpet-shaped blooms come in a wide range of colours. The plants will enjoy several hours of sun per day, but not very strong mid-day sun.

Trailing plants are, of course, ideal for shelves, including the succulent *Ceropegia woodii*, with thin stems and marbled heart-shaped leaves, purple below. It likes full sun, and in winter should be kept cool and virtually dry. The same conditions are needed by several other trailing succulents, like *Sedum morganianum*, with 60 cm (24 in) long stems densely clothed with cylindrical pale green leaves; and *Senecio rowleanus* with stems of similar length, carrying rounded grey-green leaves.

The popular trailers, tradescantias and zebrinas, are ideal for window shelves as they produce their best colours in really bright light. They are adaptable, too, thriving in warm or cool rooms.

The dwarf orange or calamondin, *Citrus microcarpa* (*C. mitis*), needs really bright light but protection from direct strong sun. A minimum temperature of 13°C (55°F) is needed in winter. It has highly scented white flowers and tiny orange fruits.

Another fruit suitable for window shelves is the dwarf pomegranate, *Punica granatum* 'Nana'. It bears scarlet flowers and small, but inedible, yellowish-orange fruits. It enjoys some direct sun, and a minimum winter temperature of 7°C (45°F).

A 'fun plant' for window shelves is the sensitive plant, or *Mimosa pudica*, much-loved by children, and most adults, too, as its pinnate leaves rapidly collapse when touched, although after a time they assume their normal position. Suitable for normal room conditions, and best raised anew from seed each year. It will enjoy some direct sunshine.

Finally, a few more coloured-foliage plants with thin leaves, through which the light will shine. All can be grown in normal room conditions and they enjoy humidity when temperatures are high. They should be protected from direct strong sunshine, though. *Coleus blumei* varieties have multicoloured foliage and are best grown as annuals, raising new plants each year from seeds or from soft cuttings. Comparatively new on the house-plant scene is the polka dot plant, *Hypoestes phyllostachya* (*H. sanguinolenta*), but it has rapidly become popular. It has deep green leaves heavily spotted and splashed with bright pink. This is best raised from seeds each year, these being sown in the spring. More popular in the USA than in Britain are the iresines, including *I. herbstii* with red foliage, and the yellow-leaved *I. herbstii* 'Aureoreticulata'. Both should be replaced regularly by young plants which are easily raised from cuttings in spring or summer.

16

ARTIFICIAL LIGHTING

I feel that not enough use is made of artificial lighting for houseplants – at least in Britain. People in the USA seem far more aware of the benefits of lighting for indoor gardening.

There are two ways of using artificial lighting: to encourage optimum plant growth and flowering, and to highlight plants purely for decorative effect.

Artificial light is used to increase natural light levels, particularly in dark corners, etc. It can also be used as an alternative to natural light, for example in cellars, basements, etc, where there may be no windows. With the right type of light, plants can thrive in completely artificial conditions.

MAKING A CHOICE

The ordinary incandescent filament bulbs which we use for room lighting are only of decorative value as far as plants are concerned. They can be used as spotlights, to highlight specimen plants or groups of plants at night. The spotlights can be mounted on the ceiling or high up on the walls and, of course, they are normally adjustable as regards angle. Incandescent filament bulbs do not substantially improve plant growth and should certainly not be placed too near plants for they give off a lot of heat which can result in leaf scorch and other damage. By the way, do not use coloured bulbs for spotlighting plants, for they create unnatural-looking effects.

If you want to provide artificial lighting for plant growth use fluorescent tubes as these give out far more light than heat and can be placed quite close to the plants. Tubes can be used to increase natural daylight in rooms, or they may be used to completely replace it –

say in cellars or basements with no source of natural light. There are several kinds of fluorescent tube suitable for use with plants. The best for plants, to ensure good growth and flowering, are 'natural white' tubes; or you could combine these with 'daylight' tubes, although the latter are not suitable if used on their own.

LIGHTING UNITS

For plants of average size it is recommended two tubes are used, set 15 cm (6 in) apart. They should have a reflector behind them to direct the light downwards onto the plants. You should ensure that the tubes are mounted in such a way that they can be easily and quickly raised or lowered, for their optimum height above the plants often has to be ascertained by trial and error. You will have to be prepared to experiment until you find the height that ensures optimum growth and flowering. If the lights are too far away, then the plants will make very spindly and weak growth, while if they are too close the tubes may scorch the leaves, and you may also notice a loss of foliage colour.

However, you will need some kind of guide. It is recommended that as a substitute for natural daylight the tubes should be set between 30 and 60 cm (12 and 24 in) above foliage plants, and 25 to 30 cm (9 to 12 in) above flowering subjects. Try these heights, too, for supplementing natural daylight.

If fluorescent tubes are the only source of light, then leave them on for up to 18 hours per day. If they are intended to supplement natural light then they can be left on for up to eight hours per day, for example in the late afternoon and evening. But it will do no harm

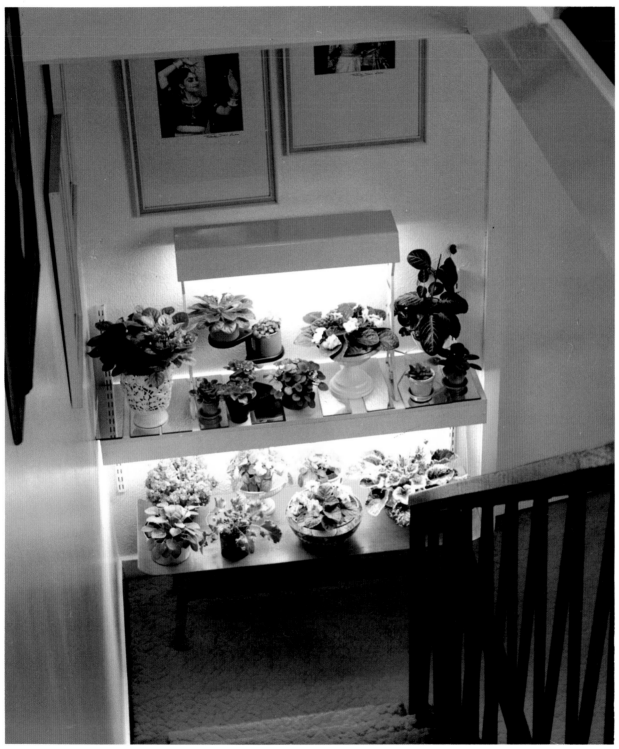

Artificial lighting allows one to display plants in dark parts of the house and also encourages them to grow and flower. African violets respond particularly well.

to leave them on for up to 18 hours, especially if they are needed to show up plants in dark or shady areas.

Of course, there is no need to be on hand all the time to switch lights on and off – there are available electric timer switches which will do the job for you.

It is important to replace fluorescent tubes once a year for after this period they are not so effective. Certainly when tubes start turning dark at the ends they should be changed. The light intensity is very much reduced at the ends when they darken.

Lighting units are best installed by a qualified electrician as it is dangerous to dabble in electricity if you know little about it.

An advantage of fluorescent tubes is that they can be installed in many places: for instance, you could, perhaps, put up several wall shelves, one above the other, with tubes mounted under each one. They can also be mounted under the covers of fish tanks (see Chapter 17).

It is also possible to buy in the UK simple proprietary lighting units for plants, although one does not have a particularly wide choice. I would suggest there is great scope for manufacturers to bring out more models, considering there is great interest in houseplants. There is a far wider choice of lighting units in America, though.

Also probably more popular in America than in Britain are plant trollies on wheels complete with artificial lighting (Fig. 12). These enable displays to be easily moved, say from one part of a room to another, or from room to room. DIY enthusiasts could, of course, easily make an illuminated plant trolley. For instance, a wooden tea trolley could be equipped with fluorescent tubes mounted under the top shelf.

The DIY enthusiast may also enjoy the challenge of constructing a tiered plant stand, with several shelves, under each of which can be mounted fluorescent tubes. Such a stand could be made to fit into the corner of a room. If you do not feel you could make such units for plant display, then take a look around furniture stores for some suitable units. There are all kinds of shelving and display units available today which could so easily be fitted with artificial lighting.

Fig. 12. A plant trolley on wheels, complete with artificial lighting, is easily moved around. This is a project for the DIY enthusiast.

17
GLASS DISPLAY CASES

Some plants are very delicate and quite unsuitable for growing in normal room conditions. They need steady warmth and constant, very high humidity. Such plants can be grown in a glass case in a warm room. Ideal for this purpose are glass fish tanks, available in a wide range of sizes from aquarium and tropical-fish centres, of which there are many in the UK. Ideally buy one complete with cover and built-in fluorescent tube, for lighting will be needed to show up the plants and it also encourages flowering. A light will also enable you to position the tank in a dark corner, and it should be on for about 16 hours per day to encourage good growth and flowering.

Do not use plastic fish tanks, for plastic is easily scratched; and it can also discolour after some years.

A glass tank, artistically planted with exotic and colourful plants, can make a stunning room feature. The idea is not new (although lighting is comparatively new), for the Victorians grew delicate plants in glass cases, known as Wardian cases or terrariums.

A planted tank can be stood on the floor, in a fireplace, on a low table, on a shelf, or even on a windowsill if it's wide enough. Do not position the tank where it will receive direct sun, though.

PREPARING THE TANK

First wash it out with water and soft soap to ensure the glass is really clean and sparkling. Allow to dry thoroughly before the next stage of preparation, which is to place a thin layer of shingle, about 2.5 cm (1 in) deep in the bottom to act as a drainage layer. On top of this place a layer of compost in which to plant. Most of the plants recommended for tanks like plenty of humus in the compost, and so the peat-based potting composts are suitable. Drainage of these can be improved by adding some perlite and vermiculite. You will need a layer of compost about 7.5–10 cm (3–4 in) deep and it should be moistened if necessary before adding it to the tank.

PLANTING

Most of the plants used in tanks are fairly low growing and once established will form a lowish carpet, resembling the 'floor' of a tropical rain forest. Many of the plants used are indeed inhabitants of tropical rain forest.

The tallest plants should be placed at the back, with perhaps a few at the sides of the tank. Then you can grade down to the front with low growers. To complete the scene you can add, if you like, a few pieces of tree branch or bark – even cork bark can look most effective. Dark brown or blackish mangrove root, which is available from tropical-fish dealers, can look most effective, too.

PLANT CARE

Once planted, a tank needs little attention. Keep an eye on watering and do not allow the compost to dry out – it should be kept steadily moist. In the enclosed conditions of a tank you will find that the compost dries out only very slowly. Humidity can be increased if necessary by lightly spraying the plants.

It is important to regularly remove any dead leaves and flowers, for if left for any length of time they could encourage the fungal disease botrytis or grey mould, which could then spread very rapidly in the warm moist environment, affecting healthy plants. If this fungus disease does appear, the plants should be sprayed with the systemic fungicide, benomyl. All affected parts of plants should be cleanly cut away first, though.

Some judicious trimming may be needed from time to time as some plants will make steady, quite vigorous growth in a tank, although it should be said that very vigorous or rampant subjects should not be included in the planting scheme, for they can swamp other plants.

Liquid feed the plants every two to four weeks in the summer, using half the recommended strength.

A CHOICE OF PLANTS

In the following list of suggested subjects, some are easily available from garden centres, florists, and the like, while others will have to be bought from specialist suppliers of tropical and houseplants.

Aeschynanthus

These are trailing plants and you may in fact find they are too large for a tank, unless you devote a tank to perhaps just one or two plants. They will certainly enjoy the warmth and humid conditions in the tank, though, and will make excellent growth. Several species are available, including *A. lobbianus* (*A. radicans*), with bright red flowers; *A. marmoratus*, with marbled leaves and greenish yellow flowers; and *A. speciosus*, with yellow-orange flowers in clusters.

Columnea

Again these are trailing plants and may be too large for a tank, unless you grow just one or two plants. Choose the smaller species, like *C. linearis*, with deep pink flowers; or some of the compact modern hybrids, like 'Alpha', yellow flowers, 'Chanticleer', light orange, and 'Mary Ann', deep pink.

Episcia

Of ideal proportions for tanks, the episcias can only really be grown in a warm humid microclimate: they are definitely not suited to normal room conditions. They have creeping or trailing stems and are low growers. The flowers are tubular and freely produced given sufficient artifical light. Most of the plants offered are hybrids of the species *E. cupreata* and *E. reptans*, and have attractively coloured leaves. Some recommended hybrids include 'Acajou', red-orange flowers, silvery green and coppery foliage; 'Chocolate Soldier', red flowers, deep brown leaves with silver main vein; and 'Cleopatra', orange-red flowers, leaves patterned with pale green, pink and white. *E. lilacina* is a beautiful species worth searching for, as it has large lilac blooms and bronzy green foliage.

Fittonia verschaffeltii

A virtually prostrate carpeting foliage plant, ideal for tanks as it will not make satisfactory growth in normal room conditions. The deep green leaves have red veins. There are several varieties of this species, like 'Argyroneura', whose leaves have conspicuous silver veins. 'Argyroneura Nana' is a very dwarf form and the one usually offered by garden centres.

Saintpaulia (African violet)

Any of these are ideally suited to growing in tanks. There is an exceedingly wide range of varieties to choose from, perhaps not in the garden centres, but certainly from a specialist. As well as the normal-sized plants, the new micro-miniatures should also be considered. They are very tiny plants and you could therefore fit quite a collection into a tank. Examples of varieties available in the UK: 'Pip Squeek', pink flowers; 'Tinkerbell', mid-blue; 'Elf', lilac; 'Sprite', white, with a hint of blue; 'Twinkle', pink; and 'Blue Imp', tiny star-shaped blue flowers. The trailing varieties of African violet are also suitable for tanks, like 'Breezy Blue', mid-blue flowers; 'Sweetheart Trail', bright pink; 'Jet Trail', blue; 'Trail Along', pink; 'Snowy Trail', white; and 'Easter Trail', deep lilac.

It is now possible to obtain some of the

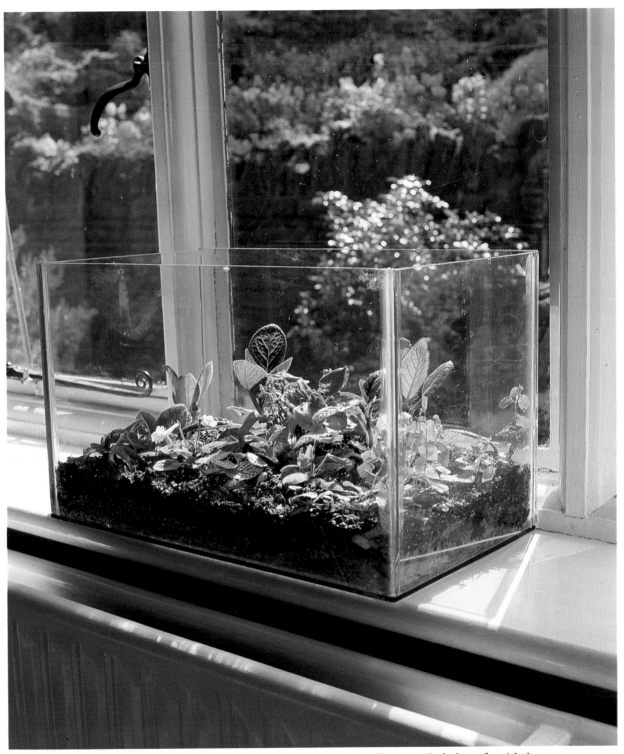

One of Mrs Barbara Potter's planted fish tanks in which delicate tropical plants flourish due to the high humidity and steady temperature. This tank contains a collection of gesneriads.

species of saintpaulia from specialist growers and these, too, can be recommended. I cannot guarantee you will find all of the following, but look out for at least some of them: *S. confusa*, *S. nitida*, *S. orbicularis*, *S. pendula*, *S. pusilla* and *S. velutina*.

Selaginella

These are foliage plants, forming low ferny or moss-like hummocks of growth. There are several species available, like *S. kraussiana*, creeping habit, green foliage; *S. k.* 'Aurea', yellow-green foliage; *S. apoda*, pale green and mossy; *S. emmeliana*, ferny pale green stems up to 30 cm (12 in) high; and *S. martensii*, erect habit, finely divided green stems.

Sinningia

Miniature sinningias are ideal for tanks, being mainly hybrids of *S. pusilla*. They form flat rosettes of leaves and produce tiny streptocarpus-like blooms ranging from lavender to violet. Available hybrids include 'Cindy', 'Dollbaby' and 'Freckles'.

Sonerila margaritacea

A low creeping plant grown for its attractive foliage. The leaves are deep green, heavily speckled with silvery white. The undersides are purple and the stems red.

A PRIVATE COLLECTION

During the preparation of this book I visited several private houseplant enthusiasts, including Barbara Potter, who is Show Secretary of the Saintpaulia and Houseplant Society. She specializes in plants of the *Gesneriaceae* family, growing them in glass fish tanks. So impressive is her collection of plants that I feel it is well worthwhile discussing it here in some detail.

Mrs Potter said that growing gesneriads in glass fish tanks is far more satisfactory than trying to create the necessary very humid conditions in a room which would, of course, lead to a very damp atmosphere.

Her tanks are not independently heated but rely on the warmth provided by the central heating. They are illuminated, though, by means of fluorescent tubes mounted in the covers of the tanks. The lights are on for 16 hours per day, all the year round. This artificial light not only allows the plants to be seen much better (it is even possible to site the tanks in quite dark corners), but also ensures the plants grow and flower well.

The growing medium in the tanks is a mixture of sphagnum peat, vermiculite and perlite, plus Phostrogen as a base fertilizer.

The plants are beautifully arranged in the tanks, some of which resemble the 'floors' of tropical rain forests. Of course, the plants are easy to arrange in fish tanks because access is so easy. Mrs Potter is not a lover of 'bottle gardens', where plants are grown in large bottles such as carboys, as it is very difficult to plant and attend to plants through the narrow opening.

Her plants are obtained from all over the world, from friends in Malaya, and from societies in America and Australia.

Most of her tanks contain episcias, creeping or trailing plants with attractive foliage and flowers, from the rain forests of South America. To develop them to their full potential they are given warm, very humid conditions and good light.

Most of the episcias are seedlings; a particularly attractive named one, though, is 'Country Caper' which has bronze foliage. Another is the species *E. lilacina*.

There are plenty of fittonias, too, plus marantas, foliage begonias and a selaginella with lime-green foliage.

Miniature sinningias are also flourishing in these warm, humid microclimates; and some tanks also contain achimenes, saintpaulias and smithianthas.

Rare and difficult plants rub shoulders with the more familiar and easier subjects, like the rare *Parakohleria abonda*, with fuzzy, red, ball-shaped flowers; *Gesneria cuniefolia* with orange flowers; and *Kohleria villosa*, the only small species, with crimson blooms, and very difficult to grow.

The little landscapes are completed, in some tanks, with pieces of cork bark, over which the plants scramble, giving a natural-looking effect.

Although Mrs Potter does not generally use large bottles for her plants, there are, nevertheless, some saintpaulias in carboys, one variety being 'Wood Trail'. During the summer these are stood in the open, front porch of the house. Mrs Potter has had the tops of the bottles cut off for easy access. She said there is no point in leaving the tops on as they make it almost impossible to plant and care for the plants.

A useful tip when planting such containers – Mrs Potter temporarily wraps the roots in cling film when planting, to avoid getting compost on the leaves of the plants, which is virtually impossible to remove from saint-paulias as they have hairy foliage.

18

MINIATURE DISH GARDENS

Groups of small plants, artistically arranged in a small container, make a pleasing centre-piece for a table, sideboard, coffee table etc. They are best vieweed either at eye level or from above.

The plants may eventually become too big so dish gardens are generally treated as temporary decorations, although they will give pleasure for about a year or so.

If you have children you may find that they enjoy making up these miniature arrangements – it is certainly one way of getting them interested in growing things.

PREPARATION AND PLANTING

Normally a shallow dish or trough is used, about 10 cm (4 in) deep. It can be made of various materials, such as china, pottery etc, provided it is waterproof – in other words, does not have drainage holes in the bottom through which surplus water can seep.

First place a layer of drainage material in the bottom of the dish or trough. Gravel, shingle or horticultural aggregate placed about 12 mm ($\frac{1}{2}$ in) deep would be suitable. Top this with a thin layer of rough peat or leafmould, to prevent compost from washing down and blocking it.

The advice given on grouping plants in Chapter 10 applies equally to dish gardens, in that all the plants used must be suited to the same conditions. They must all have the same requirements in respect of light, temperature and humidity. Also they must have the same needs in respect of watering, for the plants are actually planted in compost. It is no use growing plants which like very moist compost with those which need far drier

conditions. The advice in Chapter 10 on grouping plants for contrast and harmony applies just as much to dish gardens.

The best way to plant a dish garden is first to place a layer of compost over the drainage material and to firm it moderately. Then the plants are removed from their pots and placed on the compost, moving them around until you are satisfied with the arrangement. Then compost should be trickled around the rootballs, firming moderately as you proceed. Do ensure that the tops of the rootballs are very slightly below the final level of the compost, and leave space between the compost surface and the rim of the container for watering – about 12 mm ($\frac{1}{2}$ in) should be adequate.

After planting, water in the plants. You must remember to be careful with watering, for the container has no drainage holes and it is so easy to end up with water-logged compost. It is a good idea, a few minutes after watering, to carefully tilt the container to allow any excess water to drain off if you feel you have applied too much.

MIXED GROUPS

Choose small young plants for dish gardens and make sure they are slow-growing kinds. The following selection can be recommended, and all of them need to be grown in a warm living room. They also need high humidity, which can be achieved by mist-spraying them daily. They also need good bright light, but should not be subjected to direct sun.

There are not many small flowering plants suitable for dish gardens, but the saintpaulias (African violets) are ideally suited. Normal-

I have 'furnished' a small sitting room with a wide range of foliage plants. Note that the display extends almost to the ceiling. I don't like to waste wall space!

sized varieties can be used, but even better would be the new micro-miniatures. The African violets have an exceedingly long flowering period and come in a wide range of colours.

Of the foliage plants, we can include the cryptanthus or earth stars, with their rosettes of colourful striped or banded leaves, like *C. bivittatus* and *C. zonatus*. A small palm could be used, too, perhaps to give height, an ideal choice being *Chamaedorea elegans*. A small codiaeum with brightly coloured leaves could also be used to give height. More bushy plants are *Pilea cadierei* 'Nana', with silver-splashed leaves, and peperomias such as *P. caperata* with deep green crinkled leaves and *P. obtusifolia* 'Green Gold' or 'Variegata' with variegated foliage. Another bushy and colourful plant is *Maranta leuconeura* 'Kerchoveana' with greyish-green leaves spotted with reddish-brown.

Trailing or creeping plants can be used to cascade over the edges of the dish, like the creeping fig, *Ficus pumila*, with bright green heart-shaped leaves; and varieties of common ivy, or *Hedera helix*, like 'Adam' and 'Little Diamond', both variegated with silvery grey.

CACTI AND SUCCULENT GROUPS

Many cacti and succulents are excellent for dish gardens and generally much-loved by children (Fig. 13). As most are comparatively slow growing the display should last for a number of years before it needs renewing. Grow cacti and succulents in a soil-based potting compost, such as John Innes potting compost No. 1, to which you should add one-third extra of grit or coarse sand to ensure really good drainage.

Cacti and succulents need maximum light

Fig. 13. Succulent plants are ideal for dish gardens, and as most are comparatively slow growing the display should last for a number of years before it needs renewing. Plants here include lithops, aloe, echeveria and crassulas.

and will take, and appreciate, direct sun. Keep the plants warm in spring and summer, but cooler in autumn and winter when they are resting. A minimum winter temperature of 7–10°C (45–50°F) is recommended. Water normally in spring and summer (when the compost is drying out) but keep dry in autumn and winter. However, if during the rest period the plants shrivel unduly, then give them some water.

A cacti and succulent garden should consist of a mixture of globular, hummock-forming and columnar plants, for contrast in shape. Try to choose some free-flowering plants, too, to provide colour. Do not pack the plants in too tightly, for cacti and succulents like good air circulation. After planting, the surface of the compost can be lightly covered with stone chippings or grit, to resemble 'desert conditions'.

I can recommend the following cacti for dish gardens: *Chamaecereus silvestrii*, the peanut cactus, with red flowers; lobivia species, with yellow or red blooms; mammillarias, yellow, white or red flowers; *Notocactus ottonis*, yellow blooms; *Opuntia microdasys*, with branching pads covered in tufts of short spines; and rebutias, which freely produce red, orange or yellow flowers.

Other suitable succulents include *Echeveria glauca* with rosettes of blue-grey leaves; any species of lithops or living stones, many of which flower freely; *Euphorbia obesa*, with a fat, greyish globe-shaped stem; and haworthias, such as the white-banded *H. attenuata*.

19

MOISTURE-LOVING PLANTS

An increasing number of moisture-loving houseplants is becoming available, and these need somewhat different treatment to other subjects in respect of watering, for the compost must be kept constantly moist.

A nice idea, perhaps, would be to grow them all together, in a collection, say in a large dish or some other decorative water-holding container. They could remain in their pots, and simply stood in the container. About 2.5 cm (1 in) of water should be maintained in the container, so that the compost in the pots remains permanently moist.

When grouping together any plants do bear in mind temperature requirements. Do not grow temperate plants with tropical kinds. All the plants mentioned here need good light but they should not be subjected to direct sunshine as this may scorch the foliage. The moisture-lovers are essentially foliage plants, although some may produce flowers, but these are very insignificant.

RECOMMENDED PLANTS

The following are readily available from garden centres and the like.

Acorus gramineus 'Variegatus'. In nature this is a marginal plant, growing in shallow water. It has grassy foliage, attractively striped green and white. It is best grown in a cool room but will survive in normal living-room conditions.

Carex morrowii 'Variegata'. This is a Japanese sedge which in nature grows in wet places. The grassy leaves are striped white and green. Keep moist at all times and ideally in a cool room.

Cyperus. These are sedges, waterside and bog plants in nature. There are several spe-

cies available, like *C. albostriatus* (*C. diffusus*), which has tufts or rosettes of leaves at the top of the stems. *C. alternifolius* is perhaps better-known, and is popularly called the umbrella plant. It has a similar habit of growth to *C. albostriatus*, but is twice the height, reaching 1.2 m (4 ft). There is a dwarf form, though, *C. a.* 'Gracilis', which attains only 45 cm (18 in) in height. Grow both of these in a moderate to warm room.

The giant of the genus is *Cyperus papyrus*, the paper plant, which can reach a height of 1.8–2.4 m (6–8 ft). It is perhaps better grown on its own as a specimen plant – space permitting, of course! It has bamboo-like stems, at the top of which are carried thread-like leaves in a drooping rosette. It needs really warm conditions all year round – a minimum temperature of 15.5°C (60°F).

Scirpus cernuus (*Isolepis gracilis*). This is the newest of the moisture-lovers to become available in garden centres, chain stores, etc., and is a very attractive plant, consisting of hundreds of bright green thread-like leaves which arch over. It should be grown in a cool room.

Carnivorous plants

I have included the 'insect eaters' here for they are also moisture-lovers. They are becoming increasingly popular and one or two can even be bought from garden centres, although for a wider choice of genera and species you will have to buy from a specialist supplier.

These would also look good in a group, standing the pots in an ornamental dish or some other water-holding container.

It is the temperate kinds that are suitable for indoor cultivation, the easiest to grow being the cobra lily, *Darlingtonia californica*, with tall yellowish green pitchers (in which insects are trapped); the trumpet pitchers, such as *Sarracenia flava*, with tall pale green pitchers; and the Venus fly trap, *Dionaea muscipula*, with jaw-like traps which close rapidly when insects land on them. Most children (and adults, of course) are fascinated by this plant, which is often available from garden centres.

In spring and summer the compost should be kept wet, best achieved, as already mentioned, by standing the pots in a container with water in the bottom. In autumn and winter the plants must not stand in water, for the compost should be kept only just moist. So water as it starts to dry out. The plants should be kept cool in winter, when they will be happy in a minimum temperature of 4.5°C (40°F).

In the spring and summer the plants enjoy warm conditions and high humidity, which can be provided by spraying the plants daily. The container of water, of course, will also ensure humidity around the plants. Use soft water (rainwater being ideal) for carnivorous plants, as 'hard' alkaline water can kill them. In the spring and summer the plants enjoy airy conditions, and they certainly need very good light, including some sunshine, but shade them from very strong sun.

The plants can be potted on in spring when pot-bound, using plastic pots, although do not over-pot them. A suitable compost can be made at home and consists of a mixture of equal parts (by volume) of peat and perlite. Do not add fertilizers to the compost, but instead during the summer use a dilute foliar feed, lightly spraying the plants with it about once a month.

True aquatics

These grow completely in water and in the home it is possible to grow them in a glass fish tank – indeed, tropical-fish enthusiasts will know about them for they are an essential part of the tropical freshwater aquarium. There is a very wide range of aquatics, which grow completely under water, and they are available from tropical-fish dealers. They are planted in the gravel at the bottom of the tank.

One or two tropical aquatics might appeal to people other than tropical-fish enthusiasts, and include the water hyacinth, *Eichhornia crassipes*, a vigorous grower with rosettes of shiny leaves and pale blue flowers; and the water lettuce, *Pistia stratiotes*, with rosettes of pale green leaves. Both of these are floating aquatics so are simply dropped into the water.

Both of these plants need headroom, so you will not be able to completely fill the tank with water, especially if it is fitted with a cover and built-in light, which is recommended. You must include a water heater in the tank, to maintain a water temperature of around 21°C (70°F), or a little higher.

20

GROWING PLANTS WITHOUT SOIL

Almost all houseplants can be grown in containers of aggregate which is kept constantly supplied with water, this system of growing being known as hydroculture.

But why grow plants by this method when they are equally happy in normal pots of compost? Firstly, it does away with the problems of when to water plants and how much water to apply. With the hydroculture system all one has to do is simply keep the water reservoir topped up.

Plants do not have to repotted on a regular basis and there are no bulky potting composts to move around. Furthermore, most plants make good, luxuriant growth, provided the system is cared for properly.

I would recommend hydroculture for permanent plants only, such as large specimen foliage plants; it is certainly not worth bothering with for short-term pot plants.

Ideally you should start off with young plants that have been raised by the hydroculture method: in other words, the cuttings having been rooted in water in a jar; or rooted in aggregate in a tray, which is kept moist with one-quarter strength fertilizer solution. You could, of course, raise your own plants for hydroculture.

HYDROCULTURE SYSTEMS

Firstly the aggregate. This can be a proprietary lightweight horticultural aggregate like hydroleca; or equally suitable are pea shingle and gravel.

A simple method

For this you will need a container, ideally an ornamental type, that is able to hold water. Fill it to one-third with a liquid fertilizer solution, diluted to one-quarter of the strength recommended by the manufacturer. Place a layer of aggregate in the bottom and then position the plant centrally at a suitable height with its roots well spread out and dangling straight down. Next trickle more aggregate around and between the roots until it is virtually to the top of the container (Fig. 14(a)).

The moisture will rise by capillary action through the aggregate and so keep the plant well supplied with moisture. If desired, you could insert a water-level indicator into the container (available from good garden centres), so that you know when to add more solution. Every four to eight weeks you should pour off the fertilizer solution and add a fresh supply. Annually, the aggregate and roots must be thoroughly washed under a running tap, so this means, of course, removing the plant and the aggregate. This could be considered a disadvantage with this particular system.

Using a double container

This system is perhaps more popular, and proprietary systems can be bought from garden centres, etc. The system consists of an outer, decorative container, and a smaller inner container with holes in the bottom which holds the plant and aggregate and is suspended within the larger container (Fig. 14(b)). The plant is inserted as described for the simpler method above. In the bottom of the outer container is a one-quarter strength fertilizer solution, the level of which should be kept just above the bottom of the inner container, so that it can rise by capillary action through the aggregate. A water-level gauge is inserted in the outer container, right

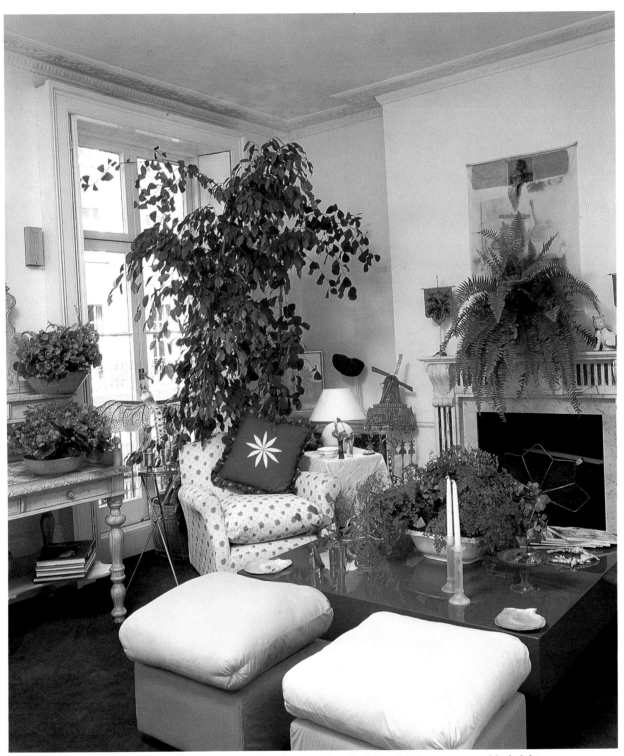

Ferns and *Ficus benjamina* create a 'cool atmosphere' while pink begonias provide bright touches of colour.

Fig. 14. The simple hydroculture system (*a*) and the more popular double-container method (*b*). The latter can be bought complete, from garden centres and shops.

(a)

(b)

down to the bottom. Eventually the roots of the plant will grow through the bottom of the inner container and down into the solution.

The solution must be completely replaced every four to eight weeks. It is also advisable at this time to wash the aggregate and roots under a running tap. This is easily done as the inner container simply lifts out, so the plant is not disturbed.

Proprietary hydroculture systems are not cheap and therefore you may wish to make your own, which is simple enough. All you need is a plastic outer container and a mesh-type pot, or even an ordinary plastic pot with extra holes made in the bottom. If you have difficulty in suspending the inner container, as in the proprietary models, it could be stood on three small blocks of wood, making sure you do not block the holes in the bottom. Again I would recommend that you buy a water-level gauge.

MOVING ON

Plants need moving to larger containers only when they have obviously outgrown their present ones. Of course, it is not too easy to remove a plant from the inner container as the roots will be growing through the bottom, so be prepared to cut these off. This should not harm the plant too much, although it may receive a bit of a check to growth until it produces some new roots.

If plants are transferred from compost to the hydroculture system they generally suffer quite a shock, so this is not generally recommended. However, if you want to try, you must first remove all compost from around the roots and then wash the roots thoroughly under a running tap to remove all further traces of compost. After installing the plant in a hydroculture container keep it warm and humid until it is obviously well-established and starting to make new top growth.

21
PLANTS IN OFFICES

Most office workers like a few plants around them to brighten the place up but offices are not often the ideal places for plants, due to a dry atmosphere caused by central heating and perhaps lack of heat at night and over the weekends. Also it is difficult to care for plants on a regular basis – they have to be left to their own devices over the weekends and holiday periods.

Very often lighting is no problem, for many offices have more than enough (for plants) fluorescent tubes overhead, and some, of course, have large window areas which let in plenty of natural light.

So the office worker is looking for really tough, adaptable plants that will stand neglect and dry air. Cost has to be considered, too. Few office workers want to spend a fortune on plants, or on watering devices that would keep them happy for a few days.

But what about watering? Certainly one should endeavour to ensure plants get enough water when the office is closed for the weekend or public holidays. Probably the least-expensive method is to buy a reasonably cheap, large shallow plastic tray in which to stand the plants. This can be lined with a piece of capillary matting. When plants are to be left to their own devices, the matting should be thoroughly wetted, even to the extent of *very slightly* flooding it. This should provide plants with enough water for a few days – they will absorb it from the matting. Also, the plants should be watered thoroughly before you leave them.

You should also buy a cheap mist sprayer so that when you are in the office you can spray the plants to create humidity around them, to compensate for the dry atmosphere, although not all plants will need this, par-

ticularly if you go in for cacti and other succulent plants, including the succulent sansevierias.

CHOOSING SUITABLE PLANTS

So which plants are capable of thriving under office conditions? I have already mentioned one or two – the cacti and other succulents are an excellent choice; and so, too, is *Sansevieria trifasciata* 'Laurentii'. Make sure you keep these plants in good light, though.

Another very adaptable plant, able to take neglect without looking too dejected, is the cast-iron plant, *Aspidistra elatior*. It can be grown in bright or poor light conditions. Attaining about 30 cm (12 in) in height, it has long, broad, pointed, deep green glossy leaves. It is worthwhile sponging these off regularly as the plant looks much better if it is not covered with dust.

Another highly adaptable foliage plant is *Chlorophytum comosum* 'Variegatum', the ubiquitous spider plant. This produces dense rosettes of arching grassy leaves, striped with white and green, and it attains about 30 cm (12 in) or so in height. In time, the plant will flower, and afterwards produce plantlets at the ends of the flower stalks.

Small plants of *Cissus antarctica* (kangaroo vine), and *C. rhombifolia* (grape ivy), are inexpensive. These plants are climbers and should be tied in to a bamboo cane, one of the least expensive plant supports. They have deep green shiny foliage which should be regularly sponged off to keep it looking good. Both will grow in shade as well as in bright light but try to avoid direct sun through the windows as this can scorch the foliage.

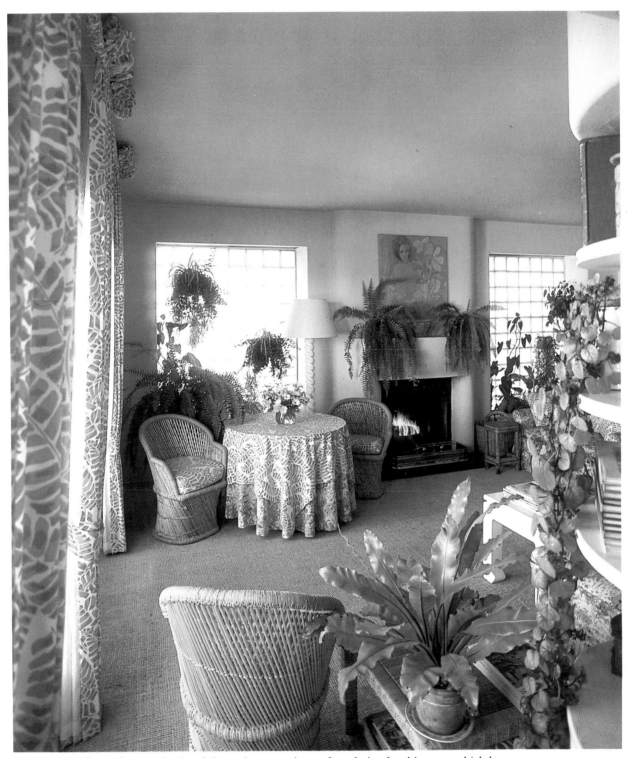

Green ferns and other foliage plants are the perfect choice for this room which has a green and white colour scheme.

The rubber plant, *Ficus elastica* 'Decora', is also very tolerant of adverse conditions and neglect and can be grown in good or poor light. Small plants, about 20–30 cm (8–12 in) high, are comparatively inexpensive. The rubber plant is so well known that it hardly needs a description: but briefly it has wide, leathery, glossy, dark green leaves carried on a single stem. Again, keep the leaves clean by regularly sponging them off.

Ivies are highly adaptable, too, and small plants are quite cheap to buy. There are many varieties, plain green and variegated, of the common ivy, *Hedera helix*; and the variegated Canary Island ivy, *H. canariensis* 'Gloire de Marengo', is a good choice, too. Grow the ivies as trailers or climbers, in shade or in good light, but avoid direct sun.

There are one or two flowering plants that will grow well enough in offices, like the popular shrimp plant, *Beloperone guttata*. This is a bushy plant which is hardly ever out of flower, producing bright pink or reddish bracts, through which appear white tubular flowers. Small plants are generally inexpensive and will be offered in flower. Try to provide the plant with bright light. The shrimp plant is a shrub so will last for several years. Large plants should be cut hard back in late winter to ensure a more bushy habit of growth. They tend to become leggy.

Finally, do try to feed the plants as this will help to ensure good growth. The least time-consuming and cheapest way of feeding plants is to insert fertilizer tablets in the compost which release their foods over a period of several weeks. Use them only in the spring and summer.

Part 4
HOUSEPLANT CARE AND PROPAGATION

22
PLANT CARE

If houseplants are to grow well and really look their best they must be given optimum growing conditions and cared for properly. They must have adequate light, warmth and humidity, and should be correctly watered, fed, potted, cleaned and, if necessary, pruned. They should also be kept free from pests and diseases. So here is a basic guide to routine plant care throughout the year.

NATURAL LIGHT

Throughout the book, and especially in the section on displaying houseplants, you will have noticed that great emphasis has been put on light requirements of plants. You will have seen that some plants need maximum natural light, including some sunshine, like many of the cacti and succulents, while others prefer to be grown in subdued light or shade, including many of the tropical foliage plants.

If light-loving plants are grown in shade they will become spindly (or etiolated) and weak, the leaves will become pale and sickly looking and the plants will not flower, or at best produce only very few blooms.

Conversely, if shade-loving plants are grown in sunny conditions their foliage is liable to become scorched or bleached.

I have indicated light requirements for all the houseplants mentioned in previous chapters. These days, most houseplants sold by garden centres and chain stores have pictorial labels which indicate growing conditions needed – do check these before you buy to ensure you can, in fact, provide the right conditions in respect of light, temperature and humidity.

If you want to be really precise you can in fact measure light intensity in various parts of your rooms by using a horticultural light meter. This is far more accurate than using your own judgement. A spot that may appear to be very light to the human eye may, in fact, have low light intensity. Some light meters are combined with soil-moisture meters (see Watering, page 110).

Of course, the greatest light intensity is to be found immediately in front of the windows, and the light is still quite bright at a distance of 60–90 cm (2–3 ft) away from the windows. These places should be reserved for those plants which need very bright light and/or sunshine.

South-facing windows have full sun for much of the day and indeed can become very hot in the middle of the day, especially in the summer. If the sun is too strong for some plants it can be diffused by means of net curtains between the glass and the plants. These should ideally be hung so that they can be drawn back on dull days. Many plants are able to take direct winter sun which, of course, is much weaker.

East and west-facing windows receive sun for a few hours per day and are ideal for plants which like very bright light, including a little direct sun.

North-facing windows receive no direct sun, but the light is very bright and does not fluctuate throughout the day. North-facing windows are often ideal for foliage plants which need very good light.

Further into a room, where light intensity is lower, reflected light from windows is a great advantage and can be achieved by means of mirrors and white or light-coloured walls, provided they actually face a window.

You will find that the leaves of many plants grow towards the light source, or the stems

This can only be described as a 'jungle room'. Philodendrons and other large-leaved tropical plants contrast beautifully with the cane furniture and blinds, and with the rush matting.

bend towards it. This becomes more pronounced the further away the plants are from the light source. If this happens, the plants should be turned regularly so that all parts receive the same amount of light. Alternatively, you can get over this problem by using artificial lighting (see Chapter 16). However, there are some houseplants, notably schlumbergeras (forest cacti, including the Christmas cactus) which should not be turned once flower buds start to appear, otherwise the buds will drop.

TEMPERATURE

As with light requirements, I have indicated suitable temperatures for the houseplants included in previous chapters, or at least indicated that they need warm, moderately heated or cool rooms. Let us firstly try to define these terms.

Warm rooms I consider warm rooms to be the living room and kitchen, where a daytime temperature of between 18 and 24°C (65 and 75°F) is often maintained, dropping at night to a minimum of 13 to 15.5°C (55 to 60°F). These conditions are suitable for a wide range of plants that need warm conditions.

Moderately heated rooms In this category I would place the dining room, bedrooms and bathroom. The maximum temperature may be around 15.5–18°C (60–65°F), with a minimum of 10–13°C (50–55°F). Again suitable for a wide range of houseplants.

Cool rooms Here I would place the hallway, staircase, landing and perhaps spare bedrooms. In many homes the dining room would also quite possibly be classed as a cool room. Possibly the maximum temperature is 15.5°C (60°F), but it may drop to around 10°C (50°F), especially at night in the hallway, etc. In the hallway, staircase and landing the temperature can fluctuate wildly due to the number of doors, and particularly the front door which may be frequently opened.

General considerations

In general houseplants prefer steady temperatures, with little difference between day and night temperatures. In most homes the temperature drops at night, when the central heating is turned down or off. However, a difference of 5°C (10°F) is perfectly acceptable to most houseplants.

It is not a bad idea to measure the temperature in rooms where houseplants are grown, using a maximum/minimum thermometer, which indicates daytime as well as night-time temperatures.

Avoid placing plants near or above radiators, heaters, stoves, etc, for it will be far too hot for them and the leaves will become scorched or dried up. A very wide shelf, though, over a radiator, will deflect hot air and can make a suitable home for plants which like a dry atmosphere.

Many tropical plants will suffer if they are subjected to very cold conditions. At all costs avoid leaving plants between the windows and drawn curtains at night during the winter, for in that space it can become extremely cold and plants may be damaged by frost. So move them further into the room before drawing the curtains.

Also avoid subjecting plants to cold draughts, from windows, doors, air-conditioning vents, and so on. The plants will become chilled and react by wilting, or dropping leaves and flower buds. Very delicate plants may expire. There are, though, as indicated in other chapters, some really tough houseplants that will tolerate even cold draughts.

HUMIDITY

The correct level of atmospheric humidity is as important for healthy growth as light and temperature. Humidity is the amount of moisture in the air and it is measured as 'relative humidity' (RH), on a scale of 0 to 100. On this scale, RH 0% is completely dry air; at the other extreme, RH 100%, the air is saturated with water. The warmer a room is kept the drier the air becomes, for the atmospheric moisture dries up. Warm, centrally heated rooms have a very dry atmosphere. In cooler rooms the atmospheric moisture is higher.

Some plants need dry air to correspond to their natural habitats, examples being many of the cacti and succulents. Other plants need moist or humid air, examples being those from the tropical rain forests. In the latter habitat, humidity can be as high as 90%, or more.

So in warm and moderately heated rooms we must provide humidity for those plants which need it (humidity requirements have been given for each plant mentioned in the previous chapters).

If we do not provide humidity plants may wilt, the result of a great loss of water by transpiration. The leaves will shrivel and may die; leaves and flower buds may drop; leaf tips and edges may turn brown.

Some warm and moderately heated rooms have higher atmospheric humidity than others, due to the nature of their use. This can apply to bathrooms and kitchens, so these may be ideal rooms for some plants which need high humidity, such as saintpaulias (African violets).

Humidity can be measured with a hygrometer or 'moisture meter'. Sometimes, this is combined with a thermometer.

But how much humidity is needed by plants? Even desert cacti and succulents, and similar plants, need some: RH 35–40% being about right. The average houseplant, which is fairly adaptable and tolerant, will be happy if the RH is around 60%. Thin-leaved or very delicate tropical plants need RH of around 80% (see Chapter 17 for examples). Obviously we cannot provide this level in living rooms so plants that need this amount of humidity are grown in microclimates, say in glass fish tanks.

Let us now consider ways of providing humidity for plants in normal room conditions. The most popular method is to stand plants in shallow plastic trays filled with horticultural aggregate, gravel or shingle. These materials are kept moist, so that humid air rises up and around the plants.

Or the pots can be placed in larger ornamental containers, such as pot holders and planters, and the spaces between filled with peat or horticultural aggregate, which again is kept moist.

Humidity can also be provided by lightly spraying the leaves of plants, using a mist sprayer. This should be done once or twice a day, depending on the room temperature. The warmer it is the more spraying needed. Never spray plants if the sun is shining on them, or it will result in unsightly scorch marks on the foliage.

Finally, bear in mind that the warmer the conditions the more humidity needed; and the cooler the conditions the less humidity. For example, in the summer, when it may be extremely hot, plants may need spraying even though they may be receiving humidity from the aggregate or peat in trays or pot holders and planters.

RESTING PERIODS

Some houseplants need a definite winter rest, for example deciduous plants (which drop their leaves), like bougainvillea and fuchsias. Most cacti and succulents also need a rest. The rest period is generally from late autumn and through the winter. At this time watering is considerably reduced, keeping the compost only barely moist, or withheld, as for cacti and succulents. The plants must not be fed and are generally best kept in cooler conditions, so it may be necessary to move them to a cool room.

Other plants, like the tropical rain-forest kinds (which include many foliage plants) do not take a rest in their natural habitats, but because we have cold winters, with very much reduced natural light, we need to partially rest them: in other words, just keep them ticking over. This is achieved by reducing watering during the autumn and winter, and by ceasing applications of fertilizer. The plants are not allowed to dry out completely, though. The required temperatures and humidity levels are, however, maintained.

WATERING

This aspect of houseplant care can cause problems for beginners, who may be uncertain of when to water plants and how much water to apply. However, the technique has to be learnt for if you keep plants too wet they could suffer from root rot and die; and if given insufficient water they will be under considerable stress and therefore will fail to grow and flower well.

As a general rule, more water is needed in the growing period (spring and summer) than in the rest period (autumn and winter) (see Resting Periods p. 109).

So, when do we water plants in the growing period? You should bear in mind that most subjects do not like the compost to dry out too much during this period.

I suggest testing the compost for moisture with a finger. Press a finger into the surface and if it feels dry on top, but moist below, then apply water. If the surface is moist or even wet, do not water.

When watering do not give a 'quick splash', but fill the space between the compost surface and the rim of the pot with water. This will ensure the compost is moistened right the way down to the bottom of the pot.

When watering in the autumn and winter, during the plants' rest period, and when conditions are cooler, watering should be reduced so that the compost is kept only slightly moist. But how do we ensure this? Again I would suggest testing with a finger, pushing it well down into the compost. If the compost is dry on the surface, and feels dryish but not completely dry lower down, water can be applied, again filling the space between the compost surface and the rim of the pot. Then leave well alone until the compost is drying out again. It is far better not to water if in doubt than to keep the compost too wet. Far better to leave the plant for a few more days, unless it is wilting.

There are soil-moisture meters available which you may care to use if you feel you cannot rely on the above method of testing for moisture content. These consist of a metal probe which is pushed down into the compost, and you read off the state of the compost from a calibrated dial, which indicates 'dry', 'moist' and 'wet'.

A word about water quality. Tap water, in many areas, is 'hard' – in other words, contains chalk. This is perfectly suitable for most houseplants, but there are some which do not like hard water, including carnivorous plants and many bromeliads, especially the 'air plants' or atmospheric tillandsias. You should use rainwater for these if your tap water is hard. It is not a good idea to use hard tap water for spraying plants, for it results in an unsightly white deposit on the leaves. If this occurs it should be sponged off. Far better to spray plants with rainwater.

FEEDING

Newly potted plants do not need feeding until their roots have permeated the new compost (usually about a couple of months), for there will be sufficient plant foods in the potting compost.

Thereafter, feeding can be carried out about once a fortnight for most subjects, but only in the growing season – spring and summer – and perhaps early autumn if plants are still making growth. Do not feed in the late autumn, winter and early spring, when most plants are resting, for they will not use the fertilizer and an excess of foods can build up in the compost, which can be harmful.

There are various ways of feeding houseplants, but the most popular is to apply a liquid houseplant fertilizer. There are many proprietary brands available, some being based on seaweed.

Another way of feeding houseplants is to use fertilizer tablets, again specially formulated for houseplants. These are about the

The restrained use of ferns creates a restful atmosphere in this living room and the pink flower arrangements echo the pattern of the chairs.

size of an aspirin tablet and are simply pushed into the compost, where they release their plant foods over a period of weeks.

Epiphytic plants which are growing on plant trees, etc, can be fed by lightly spraying the foliage with a weak solution of fertilizer, generally one-quarter of the recommended strength being sufficient.

Plants should not be fed if the compost is dry – water it first and then feed when the plants are fully charged with water. It is most important to apply fertilizers strictly according to the instructions on the packet or bottle, for you could harm plants by applying too much, or too strong a solution.

POTTING

Most houseplants make far better growth if they are potted on regularly into larger pots. If allowed to become pot-bound, when the compost is tightly packed with roots, growth will slow down considerably. Also, the compost will dry out very rapidly so you will be forever watering, and there is the risk plants will suffer stress from lack of moisture.

Having said this, there are some plants that should not be potted on regularly, either because they do not like root disturbance or, more often, because they have only a small root system; therefore small pots are adequate for their needs. Examples include the bromeliads, peperomias, saintpaulias (African violets), most of the foliage begonias, cacti and succulents.

Avoid potting on in winter when plants are resting, for they will not make new roots into the fresh compost and consequently the compost may remain too wet. The roots may then rot. The best time is in spring just as plants are starting into growth.

To ascertain whether or not a plant needs potting on you will need to inspect the roots. To do this, turn the pot upside down and tap the rim on the edge of a table to loosen the rootball, and slide off the pot. If there is a mass of roots, then pot on; but if a large volume of the compost has no roots through

it, return the plant to its present pot.

Generally plants are potted on to the next size of pot, for example from a 12.5 cm (5 in) pot to a 15 cm (6 in) pot. However, more vigorous plants can with advantage be moved on two sizes – for instance, from a 10 cm (4 in) pot to a 15 cm (6 in) pot.

The trend these days is to dispense with drainage material in the bottom of the pot. But I feel that for plants which like very well-drained conditions, drainage material should be provided (examples are cacti and succulents). I also think it is necessary when we come on to larger pots – say over 15 cm (6 in) in diameter. The traditional drainage material is broken clay flower pots, known as 'crocks'. A large piece is placed over the drainage hole and then a layer of smaller pieces placed over this. Cover with a thin layer of rough peat or leafmould, followed by a layer of compost which should be firmed. Place the plant in the centre of the pot and fill in with compost, firming all round with your fingers. You should ensure the top of the rootball is slightly covered with fresh compost, and there must be space between the final compost level and the rim of the pot to allow room for watering. This can be about 12 mm ($\frac{1}{2}$ in) for small pots and up to 2.5 cm (1 in) for larger pots.

After potting water in the plant to settle the compost around the roots.

Plastic pots are often used today, but for plants which like very well-drained conditions and dryish compost (cacti, succulents, pelargoniums, sansevierias and the like), I prefer clay pots. I also use clay pots for large plants as they are heavier and more stable.

COMPOSTS

Today we have a choice of soil-based potting compost – the traditional John Innes composts – and soilless or peat-based. It is safe to say that virtually all houseplants can be grown in the John Innes (JI) potting composts. Plants which like very well-drained conditions (cacti, succulents, pelargoniums,

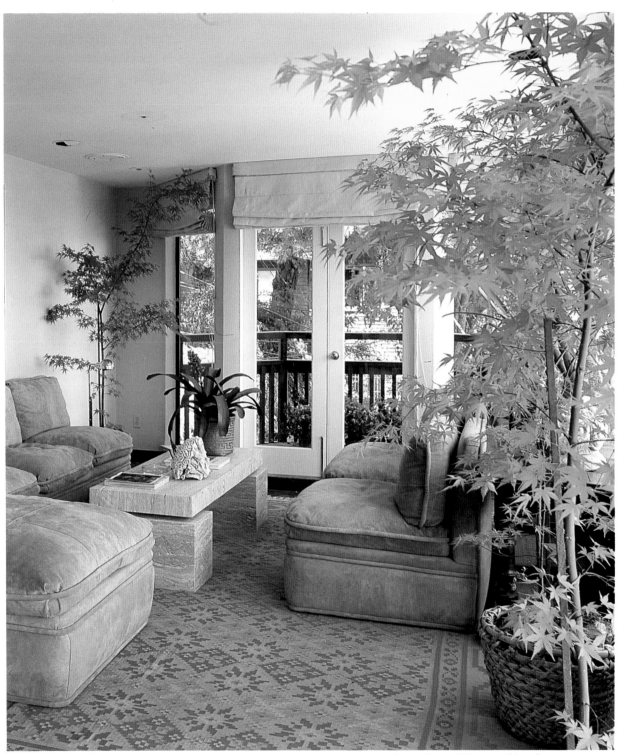

These specimen plants are, surprisingly, hardy Japanese maples and would be considered only short-term residents, but what a beautiful 'cool atmosphere' they create.

113

etc.) are certainly best grown in JI. Often I add extra grit or coarse sand to make the drainage even better. About one-third extra to a given volume of compost.

JI potting compost No. 1 is used for initial potting of seedlings and rooted cuttings, while JI No. 2 is used for potting on, as it contains more fertilizer. Very large plants can be potted on into JI No. 3 which is a very rich compost.

Other plants are happy in soilless or peat-based composts, especially those from tropical rain forests which like plenty of humus (these include the majority of our foliage houseplants). There are peat-based composts specially formulated for houseplants, or you could use a general-purpose type.

You will find in the garden centres special-purpose composts – for example, cactus composts, and ericaceous composts, which should be used for lime-hating plants like rhododendrons or azaleas.

CLEANING PLANTS

If the leaves of houseplants are allowed to become covered with dust and grime they will not function properly and growth will be adversely affected. Therefore, at least once a month, or as often as you consider necessary, leaves should be sponged off with tepid water. If the plants have hairy or woolly leaves, though, they should be dusted off with a soft brush. This also applies to cacti.

Plants with thick shiny leaves can, if desired, be treated with a proprietary leaf-shine product to make them even more glossy. Some come in aerosol form. Follow the manufacturer's instructions on use, as they are not suitable for all plants and could damage others if not used correctly.

PRUNING

If some plants become too tall, for example climbers, and shrubs like rubber plants and figs, do not be afraid to cut them back. Some plants become bare at the base as they age,

devoid of leaves, for example rubber plants and other species of ficus, dracaenas and dieffenbachias. Again these can be cut back. Beheading plants in this way generally results in new shoots being produced lower down the stem, so the plants become more bushy. This cutting back is best done spring, just as the plants are starting into growth.

Other plants need regular pruning in late winter, particularly fuchsias, bougainvilleas and hibiscus. Here the old flowered shoots are cut back to within a few buds of their base in late winter.

Do not be afraid to give other plants a trim, too, if you feel they are becoming leggy or have straggly shoots – judiciously reduce the length of the shoots to avoid spoiling the natural shape of the plants.

Sometimes variegated plants produce all-green shoots. These should be cut out completely otherwise they may take over the plant.

When pruning, always cut immediately above a growth bud or leaf, and use really sharp secateurs to ensure clean, rather than ragged, cuts, which heal much more quickly.

Some plants 'bleed' milky latex when pruned, for example the ficus. To stop this, the cuts should be dusted with powdered charcoal.

Pinching
Pinching or stopping is a form of pruning and involves removing the growing tip of stem or shoots of young plants, to encourage them to make bushy growth. Simply nip out the tip with your fingers, or cut it out with a knife, just above a bud. You need only remove 6–12 mm ($\frac{1}{4}$–$\frac{1}{2}$ in) of the tip. This will result in dormant buds lower down the stem or shoot starting into growth. Most plants that need it should be pinched initially when they are 7.5–10 cm (3–4 in) high. Then the resultant side shoots can be pinched when they are a similar length.

You should bear in mind that pinching delays flowering, so if you are growing fuchsias, for instance, remember that flower buds will only start to develop six to eight weeks after pinching.

Plants which are generally pinched to encourage bushiness include coleus, beloperone, fuchsias, hypoestes, iresine, pilea, setcreasea, tradescantias, zebrinas, gynura, plectranthus, pelargoniums, abutilons, heliotrope and impatiens.

PESTS AND DISEASES

Pests and diseases may attack some houseplants and an eye should always be kept open for signs of trouble. Indoors it is best to use an aerosol houseplant pest killer with a wide spectrum of activity. One such will eradicate common pests like greenfly, red spider mites, whitefly, scale insects, mealy bugs and thrips. To date there are no fungicides available in Britain specifically for use in the home, so if any of your plants become infected with common fungal diseases such as mildew and grey mould (botrytis) then take them out of doors and spray them thoroughly with benomyl fungicide. When dry take them back inside.

23

PROPAGATION

Many houseplants can be propagated from cuttings of various types, by division, from plantlets and offsets, and by air layering. Also, collections can be increased by raising plants from seeds, which are obtained from seedsmen.

The equipment and various other items needed for plant propagation are discussed in Chapter 1.

RAISING PLANTS FROM SEEDS

It is possible to buy seeds of foliage plants, including palms, although foliage plants often take a long time to reach a reasonable size. Short-term flowering pot plants are also raised from seeds, including primulas, cyclamen, celosias, cinerarias, calceolarias and the like.

The usual time for sowing is in the spring, certainly for flowering pot plants, although foliage plants can be sown any time up to mid-summer.

Use a good seed compost, soil-based or soilless, which needs to be light, well aerated and drained. If you are raising cacti and succulents use a soil-based compost but make the drainage really sharp by adding to it one-third extra of grit or coarse horticultural sand.

Small quantities of seeds can be sown in 9–10 cm (3½–4 in) pots or half pots; larger quantities in half-size seed trays. It is important to sow the seeds as thinly as possible – no two seeds should be touching. Seeds of some houseplants are extremely tiny – almost like dust – an example being begonia. In order to sow these evenly they should first be mixed with some very fine, dry silver sand. This mixture is then scattered evenly over the compost surface.

Very tiny seeds must not be covered with a layer of compost, but lightly pressed into the surface with a flat wooden presser. Larger seeds are covered with a layer of compost which equals twice their depth – sift it over them, using a fine-mesh sieve. The layer of compost must be of a uniform depth all over. Seeds of cacti and succulents are best covered with a layer of fine horticultural sand.

The compost should be moistened after sowing, best achieved by standing the containers in water almost up to their rims, until the surface of the compost becomes moist. Then remove and allow to drain. Instead of using plain water I would suggest you use a solution of Cheshunt Compound or a similar fungicide, to prevent damping-off disease, which causes seedlings to suddenly collapse and die.

Germinate the seeds in warmth: most require a temperature of 18–21°C (65–70°F), easily achieved in an electrically heated propagating case. Alternatively a warm airing cupboard could be used, or a warm windowsill. Unless the pots are in a closed propagating case, they should be covered with a sheet of clear polythene to prevent the compost from drying out. Keep the compost steadily moist.

Do bear in mind that the seeds of some houseplants can take many months to germinate, while others will be through within a matter of weeks.

As soon as seedlings have produced their first true leaf (as opposed to the initial 'seed leaves'), they should be pricked out or transplanted into individual 7.5 cm (3 in) pots, using JI potting compost No. 1 or an equiva-

Trailing ivies or hederas make an effective window display here. These plants are hardy and can be grown in cool rooms.

lent soilless type. Water them in after potting, again using a solution of Cheshunt Compound.

STEM CUTTINGS

A wide range of plants produce plenty of new side shoots each year and these can be used as cuttings (Fig. 15). Remove them either in spring or summer, as soon as they are large enough. Use the tips of shoots for cuttings, preparing them to a length of 2.5 cm–10 cm (2–4 in). The base of each cutting should be cut cleanly immediately below a leaf joint or node (where the leaves join the stem). The leaves should be cut off from the lower half of

each cutting, as near to the stem as possible. The bases of the cuttings should be dipped in hormone rooting powder to speed rooting – dip only the lower 6 mm ($\frac{1}{4}$ in) and knock off the surplus on the side of the container.

Cuttings are inserted in pots of cutting compost (see Chapter 1) up to their lower leaves. Make a hole for each with a pencil, drop the cutting in and firm the compost around it with your fingers. Do not pack cuttings close together – they should not be touching.

Cuttings of cacti and succulents should be allowed to dry off for a couple of days before inserting them *shallowly* in pots.

Root cuttings in a temperature of 18–21°C

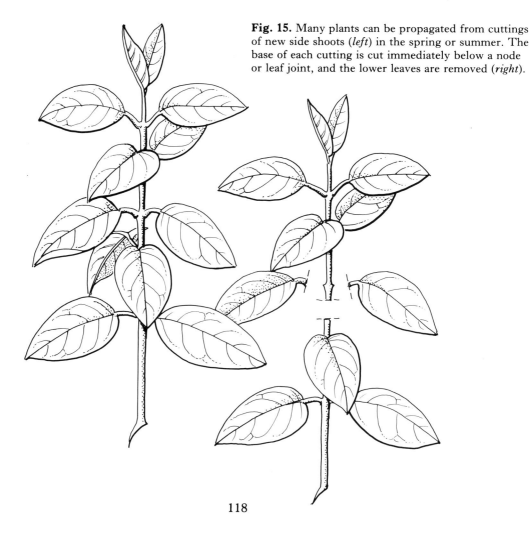

Fig. 15. Many plants can be propagated from cuttings of new side shoots (*left*) in the spring or summer. The base of each cutting is cut immediately below a node or leaf joint, and the lower leaves are removed (*right*).

(65–70°F), either in a propagating case or on a warm window-sill. In the latter case, enclose each pot in a clear polythene bag to ensure humidity (not needed for cacti and other succulent plants) and ensure it is held above the cuttings by inserting a few short thin canes in the pot. Ventilate the cuttings several times a week to allow condensation to disperse.

An indication of rooting is when the tips start into growth. Then lift and pot into small pots – say 7.5 cm (3 in) pots.

STEM SECTIONS

Some houseplants with thick stems and large leaves can be propagated from sections of young stems, examples being dracaena (Fig. 16), cordyline, dieffenbachia, aglaonema, monstera, philodendron and scindapsus.

In the spring or summer cut off a young stem, remove the leaves, and cut the stem into sections, each about 5 cm (2 in) long, complete with node or leaf joint. Treat bases with hormone rooting powder and then insert vertically into pots of cutting compost. Provide the same rooting conditions as for stem cuttings. The sections will soon make top growth, but it will be several more weeks before they produce a good root system.

LEAF CUTTINGS

Some plants can be propagated from their leaves (Fig. 17) in the spring or summer, providing the same rooting conditions as for stem cuttings.

Some plants are propagated from whole leaves, complete with leaf stalk, including peperomias, saintpaulias and rhizomatous begonias. Simply insert in pots of cutting compost up to the base of the leaf blade. Eventually plantlets will appear at the base of the leaves. If there are several plantlets, try to separate them before potting into small pots.

Begonia masoniana, B. rex and similar foliage begonias are also propagated from entire leaves, but the leaf stalk is removed. The leaf

Fig. 16. Some houseplants with thick stems and large leaves, like dracaena (shown here), can be propagated ·from sections of young stem. The dormant buds on each section quickly come into growth, but roots take longer to develop.

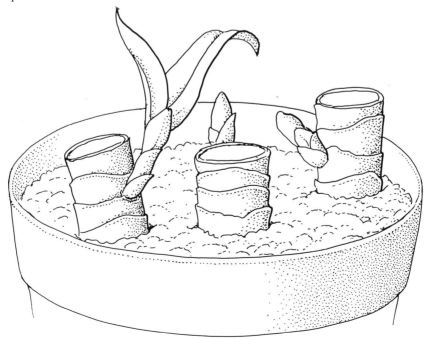

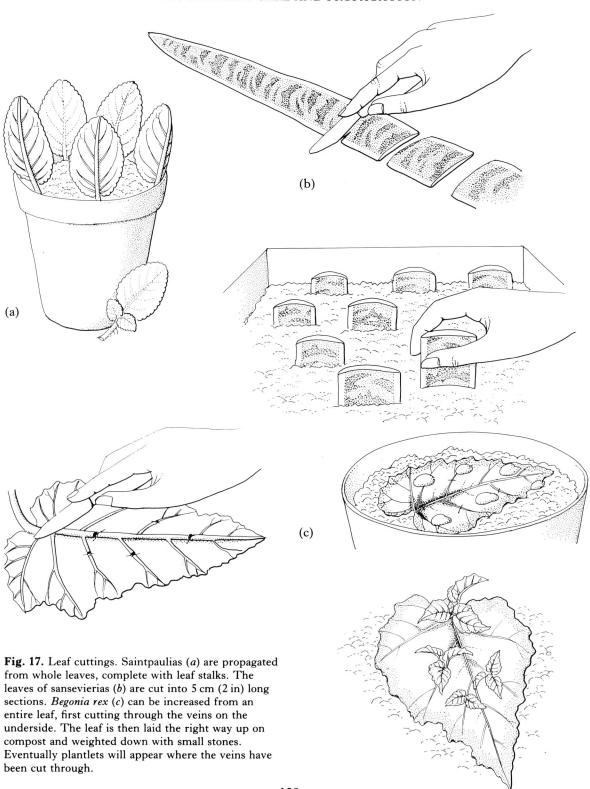

(a)

(b)

(c)

Fig. 17. Leaf cuttings. Saintpaulias (*a*) are propagated from whole leaves, complete with leaf stalks. The leaves of sansevierias (*b*) are cut into 5 cm (2 in) long sections. *Begonia rex* (*c*) can be increased from an entire leaf, first cutting through the veins on the underside. The leaf is then laid the right way up on compost and weighted down with small stones. Eventually plantlets will appear where the veins have been cut through.

is then turned upside down and, using a sharp knife or razor blade, cut through the main veins in a number of places. The leaf is then turned the right way up and laid on the surface of cutting compost. It should be weighted down with a few small stones so that the cut veins are in close contact with the compost; or you could use pieces of wire, bent to the shape of hairpins. Eventually plantlets should appear where the veins have been cut through. Lift and pot into small pots.

Other plants are propagated from sections of leaf, such as *Sansevieria trifasciata* (not the variety 'Laurentii' as the resultant plants will not have the yellow edge), and streptocarpus. Remove an entire leaf and cut it into 5 cm (2 in) long sections, ensuring you keep them the right way up. Dip bases in hormone rooting powder and then insert the sections vertically to half their length in pots of cutting compost. When well rooted and plantlets have appeared, pot into small pots.

Many succulents can be propagated from entire leaves, like echeveria, crassula, aloe and sedum. Each leaf should be inserted vertically, and very shallowly, in a pot of cutting compost, and best rooted on a warm window-sill, rather than in a humid propagator.

LEAF-BUD CUTTINGS

The rubber plant, *Ficus elastica*, and its varieties are propagated from leaf-bud cuttings (Fig. 18) in spring or summer, rooting them in the same conditions as stem cuttings. Each cutting consists of a section of young stem, about 2.5 cm (1 in) long, with a leaf at the top and a dormant growth bud in its axil. Dip the

Fig. 18. The rubber plant, *Ficus elastica*, and its varieties, can be propagated in spring or summer from leaf-bud cuttings, consisting of a section of stem with a leaf, and a growth bud in the axil. The leaf is rolled so that it takes up less space in the propagating case and the cutting is held upright with a thin cane.

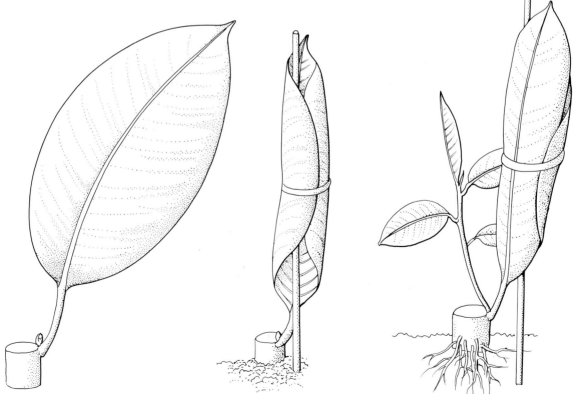

base of each cutting in hormone rooting powder, then roll the leaf longitudinally and secure with an elastic band. Insert the cutting in an individual small pot of cutting compost, burying the stem but leaving the bud exposed. Hold the cutting upright with a short thin cane pushed into the compost and under the elastic band.

DIVISION

Established clump-forming plants like chlorophytum, ferns, sansevierias, aglaonemas and marantas can be propagated by division in the spring just before they start into growth. Remove the plant from its pot and carefully pull the clump apart into a number of portions. If this is difficult use a sharp knife to cut through matted roots. The outer portions of a clump are more vigorous than the older centre part (which can be discarded) and should be potted into suitably sized pots.

OFFSETS

This is a form of division, whereby we detach new plants which form around the parent plant. Many plants produce offsets, like various cacti and succulents, and bromeliads. As soon as the offsets are large enough, carefully remove them: most will have roots so try not to damage these as you lift them. An old table fork makes a good tool for teasing away offsets. With bromeliads wait until the offsets are about 15 cm (6 in) high before removing them. Pot the offsets individually into suitably sized pots and provide warmth until well established.

PLANTLETS

Several houseplants produce plantlets (Fig. 19) which can be used for propagation. With chlorophytum, *Tolmiea menziesii* and *Saxifraga stolonifera* the plantlets can be pegged

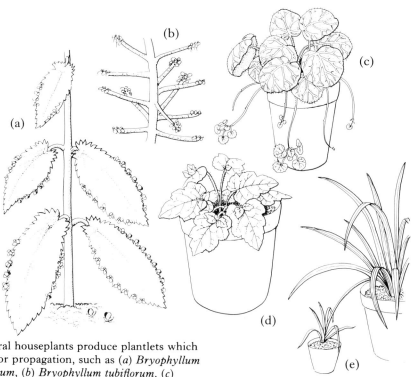

Fig. 19. Several houseplants produce plantlets which can be used for propagation, such as (*a*) *Bryophyllum daigremontianum*, (*b*) *Bryophyllum tubiflorum*, (*c*) *Saxifraga stolonifera*, (*d*) *Tolmiea menziesii*, and (*e*) *Chlorophytum comosum* 'Variegatum'.

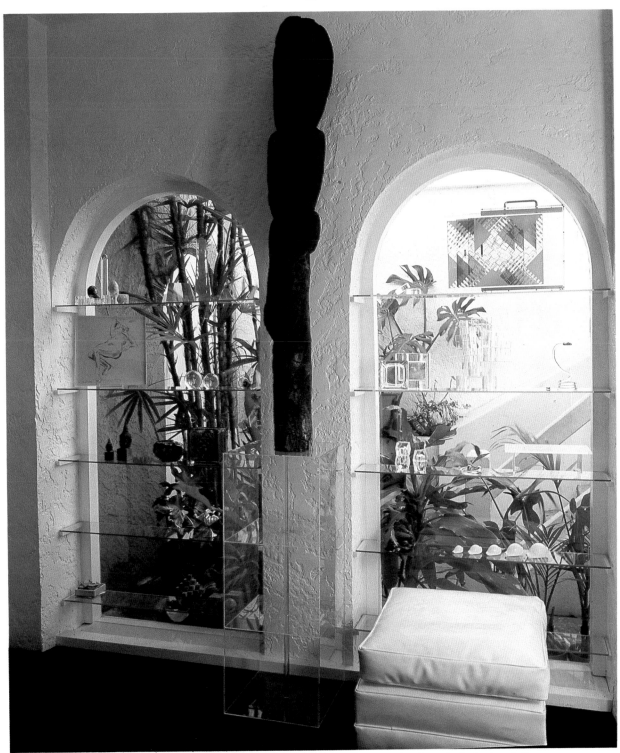

Alcoves make perfect settings for palms, philodendrons and other shade-loving foliage plants.

down into small pots of potting compost placed alongside the parent plant. Use a wire peg, the shape of a hairpin, to hold the plantlet in close contact with the compost. After a few weeks the plantlets will have rooted into their pots and can be cut away from the parent plant.

With *Asplenium bulbiferum* (a fern) remove an entire frond, complete with plantlets, lay it on the surface of potting compost and peg it down with wire pegs. The plantlets will root into the compost quite quickly, especially if kept in warm humid conditions, when they can be lifted and potted individually into small pots.

The succulent bryophyllums, like *B. daigremontianum* and *B. tubiflorum*, produce plantlets on their leaves. These are best picked off and 'pricked out', in much the same way as seedlings, into a pot of potting compost. When they have rooted and are starting to grow, pot them off individually.

AIR LAYERING

If some of your woody or shrubby plants, like *Ficus elastica* (Fig. 20), other ficus species, codiaeums, monstera, dracaenas and philodendrons, become too tall you could produce some new replacement plants by air layering. This involves encouraging the top of a stem to form roots while it is still attached to the parent plant.

The technique is quite simple. About 30 cm (12 in) down from the top of the plant cut a 5–7.5 cm (2–3 in) long tongue halfway through the stem, drawing the knife in an upward direction. Dust the wound with hormone rooting powder and wedge the tongue open with a wad of moist sphagnum moss. Alternatively remove a ring of bark, 6–12 mm ($\frac{1}{4}$–$\frac{1}{2}$ in) wide and again dust it with hormone.

Next wrap the prepared part of the stem with moist sphagnum moss, and hold this in place with a 'bandage' of clear polythene

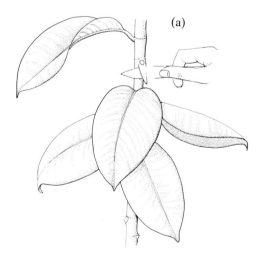

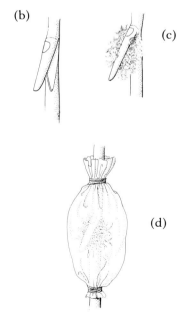

Fig. 20. Air layering a rubber plant, *Ficus elastica*. A tongue is cut in the stem near the top of the plant (*a* and *b*). The tongue is wedged open with a wad of sphagnum moss (*c*). The prepared part of the stem is then wrapped with moist sphagnum moss, which is held in place with a 'bandage' of clear polythene (*d*).

A large mirror gives the illusion of twice as many plants in this bathroom, which are displayed on plate-glass window shelves.

sheeting. Seal this bandage at both ends, and along the overlapping seam, with waterproof tape. Keep the plant in a warm room. When white roots start to show through the polythene you know the stem has produced a good root system. Remove the polythene, but do not worry about the moss, as removing this may damage roots. Cut off the rooted stem just below the roots and pot into a suitable-sized pot. Keep warm and humid until well established.

If you want to keep the old plant, it can be cut back hard – say by one-half to two-thirds – and there is a good chance that dormant growth buds will break, to give you a shorter, more bushy specimen.

INDEX

INDEX